The Occult Among Us

Exorcists and Former Occultists
Expose the Nature of This Modern Evil

by
Charles D. Fraune

The Occult Among Us

Charles D. Fraune

2024

Follow Charles D. Fraune at *www.SlayingDragonsPress.com* for news, commentary,
and publications on the topic of spiritual warfare and the Christian life.

www.SlayingDragonsPress.com
2024

Endorsements for *The Occult Among Us*

"Today, one of the evil one's most successful campaigns is that of deception, by which he ensnares souls with the offer of false spiritual goods. In his latest book, *The Occult Among Us*, Charles D. Fraune exposes the lies and the concrete dangers inherent within the many different modern occult movements through which men are increasingly being pulled away from communion with the One True God. This valuable book will be an aid to both priests and parents who seek to protect and guide their flocks in this age of increased diabolical activity."
Bishop Athanasius Schneider

"I'm proud to highlight the important work of Charles Fraune as he continues to call our attention to the evil around us. His work reminds me of the prayer to St Michael and highlights the truth that 'evil spirits prowl about the world seeking the ruin of souls.' Even as Charles helps us to face the reality of evil, he always does so reminding us that God's goodness is greater and that His Son has conquered evil. I recommend his latest book, *The Occult Among Us*, for all serious believers."
Bishop Joseph E. Strickland

"Once again Charles Fraune has written a very fine work on the occult. He unmasks the real evil of the occult and its many machinations. This is a must read for exorcists and priests in general … and for all the faithful. If I were a parent, I would have my children read this before they might be tempted to dabble in the occult, lest they do so thinking it to be harmless. The occult is springing up everywhere and this book exposes its many faces, sometimes obvious but at other times hidden. In an age and in a society in which Satan's actions are being accepted and sometimes even applauded, *The Occult Among Us* is an exposé of the true spiritual disaster that is the occult and its death-dealing fruits."
Exorcist, Msgr. Stephen J. Rossetti

Dedication

To Our Lady of Sorrows,
and to the glorious and triumphant Archangel,
Saint Michael.

For this purpose, the Son of God appeared, that He might destroy the works of the devil.

1 John 3:8

St. Michael the Archangel,
defend us in battle.
Be our protection
against the wickedness and snares of the devil.
May God rebuke him, we humbly pray,
and do thou,
O Prince of the heavenly hosts,
by the power of God,
cast into hell Satan, and all the evil spirits,
who prowl about the world
seeking the ruin of souls.
Amen.

Table of Contents

In Gratitude

A special note of thanks is given to those who willingly shared their stories for the purpose of bringing to light the active dangers of the occult as it is in our world today. Please remember them in your prayers as you read this work. A special note of thanks also goes to those priests and exorcists and laymen who shared their insights and experiences for the sake of furthering our understanding of how the devil is working within the occult and the ways in which God can liberate souls from the devil's grasp. Please offer a prayer for their continued fidelity to Our Lord. Thanks also goes to all of those who helped review this book and who offered their insights and suggestions. May God reward them for their generosity.

Preface

In my previous book, *The Rise of the Occult*, I wrote that it was the success of my first major work, *Slaying Dragons*, that moved me to compile the stories of people who, through conversion to the Catholic Faith, were liberated from the dark realm of the occult, typically with the help of exorcists and of holy and educated parish priests. The number of connections I was able to make, and the amount of information that I collected for this task, eventually became overwhelming. The sheer mass of testimony made it clear to me that, not only are far too many people being drawn into the occult, but our world is steeped in occult practices, superstitions, and philosophies.

The story that began in *The Rise of the Occult* could not be told in all its parts in just one book of manageable size. The initial research upon which that book was based created a document close to eight hundred pages long. Seeing that this would be a tome which would likely exceed what the average reader would be inclined to take up, particularly on such a serious topic, and seeing that there were numerous topics that did not fit within the narrative style of *The Rise of the Occult*, I decided to break the larger work into two parts.

With apologies to the late Paul Harvey, *The Occult Among Us* presents "the rest of the story," explaining to the reader, in greater and more practical details, what the occult today really looks like, where it is found "in the wild," and how deeply it has impacted the Church herself in this age of the world. While this book is written to be read sequentially, the reader can also treat it as a small encyclopedia of sorts, focusing on chapters that are more relevant to his personal situation. Many other readers, however, will have been impacted by the occult in some way, or will have a need to understand more comprehensively this dark religion to which people they know, or people to whom they minister, have fallen victim.

As the reader will see from the table of contents, there are many chapters that analyze specific occultic trends today. Sadly, many parents, both secular and Christian, have children who have embraced various forms of contemporary occultism. Further, many priests are now seeing that their parishioners need help in understanding just what this new occult movement is all about. *The Occult Among Us* seeks to fill this gap in knowledge by directly addressing these new movements, the dangerous social trends they are creating, and the challenges these present to the universal Church.

I have sought to present this material in a manner that respects the sensitivity of many readers and which seeks to avoid stoking unnecessary curiosity about the topics discussed. Further, I have avoided presenting details about the occult that are too dark for the imaginations and intellects of any who seek to purify and renew their minds by the working of the Holy Spirit. Being informed about the presence of this evil spiritual movement need not entail a deep understanding of what they do in the darkness.[1] What it does need to entail is a knowledge of what this religion actually believes and what these beliefs motivate practitioners to do, which then impacts both the world and the Church and, as a result, every Christian today.

Like *The Rise of the Occult,* this book relies upon the perspectives both of former occultists and of experienced exorcists in order to develop a full understanding of the spiritual situation in which we find ourselves. Further, it is informed by significant research on what occultists believe and what they seek to bring into our culture, both by analyzing what the groups say about themselves and what people are seeing them do within our society.

The Contributors

Below is a list and brief description of all the people interviewed for *The Rise of the Occult* who are also featured in this second book on the topic. As a reminder, except for Alex Frank, who has elsewhere publicly revealed his former associations with the diabolical, the names provided here are pseudonyms.

---

[1] St. Paul said, "Take no part in the unfruitful works of darkness, but instead expose them. For it is a shame even to speak of the things that they do in secret." Ephesians 5:11-12.

Preface

Former occultists:

- **Adelaide** was raised by a father who was a lapsed-Catholic-turned-atheist who later reverted, and a Protestant mother. A hatred toward God led her toward the occult. From "angel magic" she moved on to Wicca and magic, which she practiced for over ten years. She experienced strong and long-lasting diabolical retaliations after her initial weak[2] conversion to the Church.

- **Christopher's** parents left the Faith and divorced when he was young, which pushed him toward a hatred of God in his teenage years. A superstitious form of Charismatic Protestantism led him into "Christian occultism" and then into occultism in general. He endured immediate diabolical attacks upon returning to the Faith, but they were short-lived.

- **Gabriel** grew up as a lukewarm Baptist and strayed into an agnostic mindset. This led him toward New Age philosophies and practices which pulled him in and dominated his life. He endured clear diabolical retaliations as he was converting, which vanished after his entrance into the Church.

- **Camilla** was brought up Catholic but strayed into the occult while seeking healing. After witnessing the manifestation of a demon in one of her New Age instructors, she sought the Church's aid in leaving the occult. She was eventually led through a deliverance process by a priest.

- **Andrew** was raised in a non-denominational Protestant home. He left this and entered a phase as an atheist. A curiosity about the paranormal emerged and became strong, leading him into the occult. He practiced Wicca and then became a devout Thelemite for about four years before his conversion, which was followed by several months of diabolical retaliation.

- **John**, a life-long occultist, was raised initially with training in Buddhist meditation. This led to a strong and early interest in the occult. He practiced many forms of the occult for over

---

[2] She explains in the book that her first conversion, through a parish RCIA program, was without proper catechesis. For example, in her first many months as a Catholic, she rarely went to Mass on Sunday, ignorant of the obligation to do so weekly.

thirty years before his conversion. He has endured diabolical retaliation for several years, ever since his conversion.

- **Therese** was brought up as a Baptist when young and showed an extraordinary understanding of that faith at her young age. She became curious about the occult in her early teens and embraced Wicca and many forms of the occult before settling into witchcraft, Yoga, and Satanism, among others, for about twenty years. She endured diabolical attacks all throughout her occult practice. These continue today, even after her conversion to Catholicism, though with much less frequency and intensity.

- **Philomena** was raised in a lukewarm Catholic home in which her parents were seldom present. She began practicing the New Age and earth magic in her late teens, eventually marrying a Satanist. She dropped her occultic practices after almost a decade and made a soft return to Christianity, eventually entering the Church. She endured diabolical attacks throughout her practice and occasionally since her conversion.

- **Lucy** was raised as an Anglican by her parents who were otherwise lukewarm in their religious beliefs. Anger at God emerged in her late teens after her father's sudden death, fueling an emerging interest in the occult. A deep immersion into the New Age led her to a mental breakdown, which prompted a semi-miraculous conversion experience.[3] She endured strong diabolical attacks in the process of converting, but they ceased once she entered the Church.

- **Helena** was raised Presbyterian but her father was non-practicing. When she was introduced to the occult at age twenty, she was immediately drawn to it. For twenty-five years, she went from witchcraft to Dianic Wicca, back to witchcraft, and then to the New Age. Though she suffered in various ways from her time in the occult, she had little diabolical retaliation after converting.

- **Anna** was raised in the Church but began to dabble in the occult when very young. Her cultural environment inclined her toward occultic curiosities and the embrace of various

---

[3] See *The Rise of the Occult*, page 262 and elsewhere.

superstitions. By the time she received the Sacrament of Confirmation, after four years of dabbling, she stopped her occult activities. She experienced several negative events during those years, but nothing afterward.

- **Timothy** was raised by a Protestant father and a Native American pagan mother. He was not raised in either tradition but gravitated toward the pagan religion. As he began his own family, the immorality of the pagan groups he affiliated with disillusioned him, and he eventually entered the Church.
- **Barbara** was raised in a nominal Catholic home and both of her parents embraced a New Age religion. She was also raised in these occultic practices. She eventually embraced them fully and experienced numerous diabolical retaliations, particularly in the last years before she converted.
- **Alex Frank** is a former devout practitioner of the form of Yoga known as Kashmiri Shaivism who converted to the Catholic Faith in 2019. He practiced for five years and had one of the best Yoga spiritual directors in the U.S. He is also a former U.S. Army Ranger and a graduate of Yale Law School. He is now a speaker on the dangers of Yoga.

The following priests are pastors and exorcists, many with additional diocesan responsibilities. They are given the pseudonyms listed below:

Exorcists:
- **Fr. Alphonsus**
- **Fr. Athanasius**
- **Fr. Cyprian**
- **Fr. Ambrose**
- **Fr. Blaise**
- **Fr. Sebastian**
- **Fr. Anselm**
- **Fr. Matthew**

Pastors:
- **Fr. Gregory**
- **Fr. Louis**
- **Fr. Theodore**

- **Fr. Bartholomew**

In addition to the above, I interviewed numerous laymen who are not former occultists. Many only appear once, so their names are not listed here. The following individuals are referenced more than once in the book, and provided here for ease of reference as to their background:

- **Felicity**, a "seer"[4] who, due to her Church-approved spiritual gifts, works with priests and exorcists in her diocese.
- **Dr. Luke**, a licensed clinical mental health counselor. He works with young people and is used by exorcists to help evaluate their cases. He is referred to as "Dr." for ease of association to his work.
- **Elizabeth**, raised in a devout Catholic family and has remained a devout Catholic herself. Through various circumstances, she became trapped in a relationship with an abusive Satanist named **Damien**, in which she suffered for close to a year before escaping. She has worked with an exorcist for deliverance issues for many years.
- **Clare**, whose parents were Catholic but whose father was nevertheless engaged in many forms of the occult. From a young age and for decades she experienced diabolical attacks, even into her own marriage and family. Her husband's name is **Lawrence**.
- **Marianne**, a devout Catholic mother.

In addition to these personal testimonies, I consulted numerous witchcraft websites in order to gather data on the beliefs of practicing witches and to compare them to the statements of former witches. These sites are often not referenced in the footnotes, lest this publication generate unwanted attention for, or curiosity about, them, which is not the intention of the book.

---

[4] A seer, in this case, is a layman who has been recognized by the local Church to have a spiritual gift. These gifts vary as St. Paul describes in I Corinthians 12.

Introduction

Like a new "evangelical" religion, the occult has in our day spread into politics, entertainment, education, irregular medical practices, retail, social media, and, in general, into many people's way of life. It has not simply bewitched the secular members of society but has deceived many Christians of various persuasions. However, it is not new, but is an ancient deception which appears to have found a moment in the history of the world where it can easily return and stir a renewed interest. As a result, it is important for Christians, especially priests and those involved in education, to acquire an understanding about the many contemporary occult practices. The darker details are typically neither necessary nor recommended, unless a loved one or parishioner has fallen into those specific practices. However, as *The Rise of the Occult* has depicted, it is easy for a dabbling New-Ager to progress from the *soft* and seemingly innocuous occult practices to the *dark* and more clearly demonic ones.

As the reader will see from the table of contents, there are many chapters in this present work which analyze specific occultic trends today. Sadly, many parents, both secular and Christian, have children who have embraced some of these. Further, more and more priests are seeing that their parishioners need help in understanding just what this new occult movement is all about. As one pastor told me, it is absolutely necessary that Christians be able to discuss these matters beyond simply the "that's bad" surface-level engagement in the conversation.

Awareness and Wisdom

Among the benefits from learning the basics of occult belief and practice is that this awareness destroys the mystique and the fear which the occult tends to generate. Many wayward souls find the occult fascinating and alluring because of the surface-level mysticism

1

and apparent esotericism. However, when a person looks beneath the surface, or delves behind the claims, it becomes clear that the occult is not what it advertises itself to be. Further, the first thing that emerges within most people when they hear "witch" and "Satanist" is fear. However, for Christians, this fear is unwarranted. The power of Christ has destroyed the power of the occult. Faithful Christians need not fear the spiritual threats of either the diabolical or of witches and Satanists.

With a basic understanding, it becomes clear that modern occult religions 1) are not real religions but are contrived by man with the help of demons, 2) are not very different from each other despite the surface images, which make it seem like there is a wide variety; and 3) and are all motivated by the same underlying beliefs. It also becomes clear that, given that they are all basically the same, they are all also dangerous to the practitioner and dangerous to society wherever they become established. Regardless of their origin or system of rituals, the danger remains because, however more or less elaborate, like the Ouija board or the "Charlie Charlie" game, any calling upon spirits is gravely sinful and exposes the individual to serious spiritual harm, including extraordinary diabolical activity, enslavement to occult powers, and, ultimately, damnation.

A Balanced Knowledge

For those who care about the direction of the culture, and about how to stop its full plunge into the panoply of disordered behaviors that we see ensnaring this generation, it is critical that they understand just what the occult is up to, how public it is becoming, and how tied-in the occult is with this new age of immorality, exemplified by abortion and sexual deviancy, which are now pillars of the culture. It is important that Christians, and the public at large, become aware that these are central to, and often ritualistically intertwined with, the false liberation that the occult offers and which its adherents embrace.

Not all of the *activity* in the occult is occultic *rituals*. Much of this activity involves occultic ways of *thinking*. That such ways of thinking have infiltrated society, and even the Church, should serve as a wakeup call for many so-called Christians today who have "progressed" beyond Christ or have augmented His image to fit their own personal disorders and cravings for pleasure and control.

Who will benefit from *The Occult Among Us?*
- Those who wish to be able to evangelize the modern pagan world and respond properly when someone seeks out a Christian for help breaking free from occult affiliations.
- Those who want to understand why abortion and sexual deviancy are so difficult to stamp out.
- Those who want to understand what someone is actually doing when they admit to practicing witchcraft or trying to harness or channel "energy."
- Those who want to be ready to help someone who reveals that they were taught to "make friends with their demons" in order to achieve peace or enlightenment.

A further understanding of what occultists do and believe will make it very clear just how full the occult is of parody, mockery, and the counterfeiting of the One True Faith. It is always seeking to corrosively fill the void in the soul left by the abandonment of Christ by the culture. With the embrace of the occult by many sectors of society, the devil is creating a "masterpiece" of religious debauchery and is indoctrinating the culture quite successfully, if not surreptitiously. We must understand this in order to defeat it and to rescue those souls who have come into its iron grip.

As I mentioned in *The Rise of the Occult,* the Church and all Christians in union with her, as members of the Mystical Body of Christ, have a role to play in the salvation of souls. In union with Christ and as temples of the Holy Spirit, Our Lord is capable of working through us for the good of souls. Pope Ven. Pius XII, in his great encyclical, *Mystici Corporis Christi,* explained this wonderful truth. Our union with Christ makes us "His associates" in the work of salvation. The prayers, penances, and good works that we perform in a state of grace are actions of the Mystical Body, the Church, in union with the Head, which is Christ. Thus, Christ acts through us, His Body, by His inspiration and sanctifies our holy deeds, taking them up Himself and offering them to the Father. These, as Pius XII said, by Christ's will, enable the outpouring of additional graces and spiritual helps for those seeking to navigate this fallen world.[1]

May this more complete understanding of the darkness into which many of our neighbors, acquaintances, friends, and even family have fallen spur us on to deepen our life of prayer and good works that we may become, like St. Paul,[2] true imitators of Christ and, also like St. Paul, help break our world free from the darkness of sin and the lies of the Evil One.

---

[1] *Mystici Corporis Christi*, 14, 44, 106.
[2] 1 Cor 11:1.

Chapter One

The Lure of the Occult Within Fallen Man

Though the occult is a collection of apparently diverse elements, distinguished by the names of different practices, within these occultic disciplines there really is very little difference. Whether it is magic, the New Age, Wicca, Satanism, paganism, "white magic," astrology, Ouija boards, or divination – it is all the same thing when you look at the mechanism at the core: mankind's effort at becoming gods through the agency of hidden powers, energies, or spirits.[1]

The first act of magic was Adam's and Eve's eating the forbidden fruit, believing that by doing so, they would become gods. St. John Chrysostom said that the desire for the fruit was a superstitious act, which later moved to magic. "Once they move from the superstitious desire to the actual act of taking and eating the fruit, we can say that this is the first attempt at magic," which Fr. Cliff Ermatinger defines as "the attempt to manipulate powers above human nature."[2] It was not simply an act of defiance of divine law but the self-centered pursuit of deification by their own efforts through the superstitious act of eating fruit from a tree. Further, as with all occult practices, it was done at the prompting of the Evil One who made lofty promises about what would result from this act. The serpent was correct in that their eyes were opened, but his lie was uncovered when they did not therefore *see* what they expected and did not become the *gods* he had promised. He merely gave them a semblance of the Truth in which he had laid his poisonous snare, giving them their moment to chase after evil according to their own wills...and sin.

---

[1] "Becoming gods" means a lot of things, ranging from literally attaining godhood to having what would be regarded by all as god-like qualities, such as the power to change your life (and that of others) in the manner you see fit. Cf. Gen 3:5.

[2] Fr. Cliff Ermatinger, *The Trouble with Magic* (Padre Pio Press, 2021), 4.

Fr. Ermatinger explains that the Fall quickly produced a disconnect from right worship of God, as we see in the story of Cain and Abel. Since man is by nature looking for truth, meaning, happiness, and immortality, the Fall became the point of initiation for disordered worship, superstition, and idolatry, where man gives to created things what is due only to God, or looks at God through the lens of fear, as a result of the distance man now perceives from Him. "There is a snowball effect of idolatry and magic on all of mankind, so that no culture, civilization, or time has been without its own particular forms of magic and idolatry."[3]

What man is seeking through the occult is "to obtain, or mitigate, through illicit means, alleviation [*sic*] from the four effects of the Fall as well as restoration of what was lost in the Fall."[4] When man fell in Adam, he incurred four effects, each of which impact human nature itself and are inherited by all those who are born on this Earth, except for Our Lord Jesus Christ and His Most Blessed Mother.

The four effects of the Fall are a darkened intellect, the disordering of our passions (concupiscence), sickness and death (mortality), and a proclivity to malice. As Fr. Ermatinger explains, magic seeks to supply a fix to the darkened intellect by claiming to be able to grant knowledge of the future or of hidden things in the present. It seeks to fix concupiscence by offering healing or the alleviation of suffering and anxiety, to find love, to obtain cures, to obtain money and power, as well as to obtain supernatural and preternatural abilities. Magic seeks to overpower our mortality through the promise of immortality and bring health through occult practices. Regarding our inclination to malice, magic suggests recourse to curses and spells, offering therein the ability to put that malice and anger, and the desire for control over our lives, into operation and move them from a mere longing into action.[5]

Magic and occult practices have been around since the beginning of time. Camilla echoed this same truth. She said, "Basically the New Age is not new at all. It's as old as the devil himself. It's the oldest trick in the book, and that is to lie as closely

---

[3] Ermatinger, *The Trouble with Magic*, 64.
[4] Ibid 6.
[5] Ibid.

to the Truth as possible, that we might be seduced." The Old Testament is filled with the drama of idolatry, sorcery, magic, curses, amulets, divination, and the like. Even in the New Testament, we see a world saturated in occult practices, against the backdrop of which Our Lord appeared as a mysterious figure whose power was very different from that of the pagan nations. Jew and pagan alike struggled to understand the fact that Our Lord was not working with the devil to perform His signs, nor was He simply a powerful magician, but was the true God in the flesh Who acted with divine powers alone.

St. Thomas Aquinas and St. Augustine, among other Doctors of the Church, both discussed the practice of magic in their writings. Saint Thomas says that magic is a parody of God the Father bringing everything into existence through the divine Word (*Logos*). In this sense, it shows itself to be a sort of *anti-Logos*. Magic, as a result, uses evil *words* in its attempts to "bring their nefarious designs to fruition as well as counterfeit the inspirations of the Holy Spirit in the life of the human conscience." St. Augustine also speaks about the use of rituals and symbols in magic, through which demons are drawn to men, granting them favors, in an effort to win them over to a life in the occult.[6]

Today, when the gravest of immoralities are literally paraded in the streets as if they were the source of some new liberation, the wounds that emerge from the resulting sin and despair are calling the secularized world to seek out these age-old demonic remedies. The fact that the occult is surging should be seen as a predictable consequence flowing from the irreligion and debauchery by which modern man's life is too often characterized.

---

[6] Ermatinger, *The Trouble with Magic*, 119.

Chapter Two

Witchcraft and Wicca

Modern practicing witches and Wiccans admit that many of the rituals, beliefs, and practices of the modern occult do not flow from ancient beliefs and practices. This is also true of modern Satanism and the New Age, which take their inspiration from a movement that began only about a hundred years ago. This is important to know because it disperses the "sacred mist" that hovers over these spiritualities and can help dissuade the gullible and naïve who, after realizing these are but modern contrivances, will then be less intrigued by them. While the occultic systems themselves are *modern* inventions, there is still an ancient power residing within them, as there has been throughout history in other forms of the occult, since the agency operating within them is the same as the one which first tempted Adam and Eve, and which will gladly operate within any false religious framework that we provide.

The histories of modern magic, Wicca, and witchcraft are all bound together and associated with the same key personalities in the early 20th century: Margaret Murray, Gerald Gardner, and Aleister Crowley, three names that must be known in order to understand what this occult religious movement is all about. Many other occultic movements also find their inspiration and influence here.

Margaret Murray and Witchcraft

In 1921, Murray published *The Witch-Cult in Western Europe*, a book seeking to prove that the witches persecuted throughout European history were actually part of a definitive religion with rules, beliefs, and an organization as highly developed as any other religion. Her book's popularity led to her writing the entry on "witchcraft" for the Encyclopedia Britannica in 1929. This entry remained for forty years until it was replaced in 1969. One witch

YouTuber, whose videos often focus on both the history of Wicca and witchcraft as well as their modern practice, said, when discussing this entry and the existence of an historical witchcraft that had been handed down to the present age, "It is not known whether this [information in the entry] is true or false."[1]

Adam Blai[2] said that Murray, basing her ideas on statements supposedly made by witches many centuries ago about a horned god, "devised the entire religion in her imagination."[3] Statements of these witches, he pointed out, were obtained under torture and duress, so the information is not really trustworthy.[4] Though the Encyclopedia Britannica published her theory and kept it in print for forty years, he said she was eventually discredited in the academic world, which realized she had made huge leaps and conclusions on little to no evidence. Only a few did not discredit her, but all those who had real academic standing did so, he explained. As a result, the Encyclopedia Britannica stopped running her theory and now states it to be discredited. Along the way, however, Blai added, her theory was received as if it were authoritative. This was before the internet and at a time when people could not easily investigate the matter themselves to test its veracity. For forty years, it had an impact on society, forming the majority understanding of what witchcraft really was.

Murray had also found inspiration from the works of K.E. Jarke and Charles Leland. Leland's book, also disputed by historians, as witches will admit, spoke of the existence of a group of pagan witches in Italy around the 14th century.[5] More importantly, and to illustrate how intertwined witchcraft and Wicca are, Leland's book helped inspire the creation of Wicca itself. It was so influential that the name of the book, *Aradia, or the Gospel of Witches*, was adopted by

---

[1] Francisco Huanaco. "Is Wicca and Pagan the Same? Differences Between Wiccan and Neopagan." *YouTube*, May 25, 2020, youtube.com/watch?v=Vtln5rX2WMA.

[2] Catholic layman and Peritus (expert) of religious demonology and exorcism for the Diocese of Pittsburgh, Pennsylvania, whose long experience assisting with exorcisms has led to him also being a prominent teacher to exorcists today.

[3] Adam Blai's comments, here and throughout the book, come from his presentation to the 2019 Ignited by Truth conference. See video link in the References section. *EWTN*. "EWTN on Location - 2019-10-26 - Allure and Truth About Wicca and Witchcraft (The)" *YouTube*, 26 October 2019, youtube.com/watch?v=FCf7JJ4w0dc.

[4] Blai video.

[5] Cf. *The Pomegranate, The International Journal of Pagan Studies*, "Who was Aradia? The History and Development of a Legend." February 2002.

some Wiccans as the *name* for the "Great Goddess, the moon goddess."

Gerald Gardner and Wicca

It is Gerald Gardner however, not Charles Leland, who is considered the "Father of Wicca." His path, prior to creating Wicca, began with research about indigenous religions and trances. He eventually got connected to a group of Freemasons and joined the New Forest Coven, a form of witchcraft that combined Freemasonry and indigenous religions, such as Druidism, which lack adequate historical data. When he encountered the New Forest Coven, a nudist group, he thought it was so similar to what Margaret Murray described in her writings that he became convinced it was the religion she had written about. However, according to Blai, further research has indicated this is not the case. Murray had simply created, contrary to true history, and popularized a belief about an ancient witchcraft religion, one which has endured into the modern era.[6]

According to Blai, Gardner was also a close friend of the infamous Aleister Crowley, who wanted Gardner to take over leadership of his Thelema religion after his death. Gardner borrowed heavily from Crowley's dark magical rituals. Any connection with Crowley casts an even darker cloud over all of modern Wicca and witchcraft.[7] Former Yogi, Alex Frank, said that Crowley was the most powerful and influential occultist in the past few hundred years. According to Frank, Crowley believed he was receiving revelations from Egyptian gods. Crowley started his occult practice with advanced tantric Buddhism and neo-pagan religions. He was also influenced by Yoga and a lot of his occult abilities came from studying Yoga. He infused Yoga with neo-pagan practices, and the current form of Yoga that we are dealing with today has been influenced by his occult and neo-pagan ideas. Crowley, he added, was also a cocaine addict and a frequenter of prostitutes, as well as a supporter of Nazism and communism.

---

[6] Blai video.

[7] Not that *ancient* witchcraft was good. The point here is that, since the origin of modern witchcraft is connected to an evil man, Wicca and witchcraft are clearly tainted by that association.

Gardner's creation of Wicca was the result of his effort to create a modern witchcraft, a combination of all of his occult experiences, ranging from the Rosicrucians, the Hermetic Order of the Golden Dawn, the New Forest Coven, and Crowley's dark magic, among others.[8] Practitioners of this witchcraft were to be called "wiccans" even though the religion was witchcraft. This became known as Gardnerian Wicca. A lot of time is spent today by modern Wiccans and witches in the effort to clarify that these two religions, Wicca and witchcraft, are not the same thing. They admit, though, that they can be, and often are, mixed together.

Gardner and Crowley eventually split over Gardner's desire to be more public about the magical system he had created. As a result, Gardner began to publish books on Wicca and even did a BBC interview, in which he presented so-called "real living witches" to the modern world for the first time. Gardner's publicity also added credibility to Margaret Murray, a credibility very much undeserved. He claimed to have found living evidence of Murray's teachings on witchcraft. As Blai said, this began to reinforce a false authority that had begun to be given to Murray and her claims.[9]

Wicca is Invented

One former occultist, Adelaide, told me, very bluntly, "Wicca is completely made up!" Just so the reader doesn't think this statement is the distorted perspective of someone bitter as a result of what they suffered as a Wiccan, listen to Lola, a practicing witch with a huge fanbase on the internet. Lola said, "A lot of people do consider the practices of Wicca to be ancient because it does have some of that pre-Christian spirituality in it but, formally, it was only considered to be a religion, and is often considered to have been created, in the late 1930s, and was released to the public in the 1950s." Lola also added that, though it began as a British movement, Wicca now has thousands of different forms, all under the "Wicca" umbrella. Autonomy has been an intrinsic element of this spirituality from the beginning. Gardnerian Wicca, for example, had no central organization or authority that exerted control over the rituals or

---

[8] Blai video and Francisco Huanaco, *YouTube* May 25, 2020.
[9] Blai video.

beliefs in the religion. Each individual wiccan was taught to keep his own "book of shadows," or book of spells, and add to it as he developed it. This is still the practice today. Thus, each wiccan follows his own personalized version of witchcraft.

Another important figure in modern Wicca and much of modern witchcraft is Doreen Valiente, known in the Wiccan community as the "mother of modern witchcraft." Having originally worked with Gardner as his "high priestess," she left him and started her own coven of witches, which was more female-centered than Gardner's system.[10] Valiente is important because she is the one who created the famous *Wiccan Rede*,[11] the governing code of conduct for Wiccans. The *Rede* is a poem, of which eight words are the most famous, *An ye harm none, do what ye will*, these being what is typically referred to as the *Wiccan Rede*. It is not ancient by any stretch of the imagination, having been publicly mentioned for the first time in 1964 by Valiente. The *Rede* bears a striking similarity to Crowley's infamous line, *Do what thou wilt shall be the whole of the law*. This is clear in the statement of one witchcraft website, which said, "In Wicca there are no believers, there are only practitioners, people who discover that True Will is Love." This contains an important phrase reminiscent of Crowley as well, who said, "Love is the law, love under will," and taught that the "True Will" was the governing calling in a person's life, that thing toward which one is directed when they fulfill "do what thou wilt." These overlaps demonstrate that the same Luciferian belief which proclaims, *"I am god"* (i.e., "my will is Law") animates both Crowley's Thelemite religion as well as Wicca.

It's Invented and They Know It

The witch in the video mentioned above openly admitted that Wicca and witchcraft were invented but then sought, unconvincingly, to dismiss this important admission by stating that it is a problem common to all religions.[12] Reviving old religions is called "reconstructionism," he said, admitting, "Sometimes it's based

---

[10] Blai video.
[11] "Rede" is an obsolete English term that means "counsel, advice."
[12] Francisco Huanaco. "Is Wicca and Pagan the Same? Differences Between Wiccan and Neopagan." *YouTube*, May 25, 2020, youtube.com/watch?v=Vtln5rX2WMA.

on historic facts and sometimes it's fiction." This process has been described as "a synthesis of historical inspiration and present-day creativity. So," he concluded and suggested, "when someone tells you that Wicca is a made-up religion, you can proudly say, 'Yes, just like every other religion'." While we understand his desire to belong to something real, substantial, and effective, just because every religion has a *beginning* does not mean every religion is *invented*. Man-made religions are *invented* in the course of some peculiar circumstances, typically developing over centuries. The One True Faith, however, was "invented" (i.e., brought into existence), by the activity and personal intervention of Jesus Christ, God made Man. The founder of a religion establishes its meaning and power, so we must shun religions that do not have God as their author, for man himself cannot craft, i.e., *invent*, a religion that properly fulfills all of man's duties to God, to his soul, and to his neighbor, and that teaches without error the truths necessary to understand the meaning of life and the destiny of the soul.

The absurdity of religiously adhering to a modern system clearly invented by men is also not lost on other occultists. Zeena Schreck[13] said, "The so-called Pagan religions are practiced today with no regard for historical accuracy, blinded by politically correct romanticism. I'd be all in favor of bringing back the genuine Dionysian bacchanal, the Roman Lupercalia, or the Aztec ceremonies of Tezcatlipoca. I prefer the real thing to the watered-down tree-hugging that passes for Paganism now."[14]

Witchcraft vs Wicca

As already mentioned, Wiccans and witches spend a lot of energy distinguishing themselves from each other. In one of her videos, Lola explained how witchcraft is different from Wicca. In Witchcraft, there are no deities and no religion, though you can choose to add those if you would like. A witch can be non-religious or have added witchcraft to the specific religion they already follow.

---

[13] As a reminder to the reader, as was discussed in *The Rise of the Occult*, Zeena Schreck, formerly Zeena LaVey, is the daughter of Anton LaVey, who was the founder of the Church of Satan. She eventually renounced her last name and all forms of Satanism.

[14] *CUIR Underground*, issue 4.2 – Summer 1998, "Sado-Magic for Satan: An Interview with Zeena Schreck." Accessed via Zeena.eu, via Archive.org.

Witchcraft is "a craft, a practice," she said, and not a religion in itself. Witches are not a special species, she clarified. A witch is one who practices a *craft*. "It is something you learn and develop," she said, "Witches are different only because they know the craft[15] and how to use it." The time it takes to "become" a witch varies greatly and is only based on personal comfort.

Lola, who identifies as a "Celtic," discussed being Celtic and what that does and does not mean. "I would consider myself a Celtic pagan because of the deities I follow even though I don't follow a set regimented religion." She admitted that paganism today, like Wicca, "is not the same as it was thousands of years ago," but witches are simply "pulling parts of it into [their] spirituality today."

Many Wiccans will include witchcraft in their spirituality and call themselves *witches*, but every Wiccan is different. Wiccans, according to Lola, can often get pushy toward witches, forgetting that the two groups don't follow the same rules. The Wiccan avoidance of cursing, for example, is pushed on the whole witch community, though the avoidance flows from the *Wiccan Rede* and the Wiccan *Rule of Three*, which non-Wiccan witches do not follow. "This is not *all* Wiccans," she added, stating, "I have met amazing Wiccans that allow people to believe whatever they want." Being a Wiccan is not the only way to be a witch, she said, and it is not even the biggest way. Wiccans often pride themselves on having a few arbitrary moral rules but, as the stories of former occultists demonstrate, the *arbitrary* nature of these moral rules leads many Wiccans occasionally to set those rules aside or to advance entirely to darker forms of the occult which, like Wicca, also put the "do what thou wilt" of the practitioner at the center of everything.

---

[15] "The craft" refers to the practice of witchcraft.

Chapter Three

The Activity of Witches

A prime indicator of the rise of the occult in the culture is an increase in the activity and public presence of witchcraft. In recent years, there has been an increase in this very thing. In June 2020, during the explosion of riots throughout the US, witches joined the movement of chaos and hexed police officers and cast protection spells over protestors.[1] Within five days of witches joining this movement, the *#witchesforblm* hashtag had ten million views on TikTok. Even before that, in 2017, after Trump was inaugurated as President, witches crafted a spell to bind him and continued to do so every month. It became so popular that thousands of witches were estimated to have taken up the ritual spell that had been crafted for this purpose, including a singer named Lana del Ray, who is reported to have joined other witches casting the spell publicly, in front of Trump Towers.

Nearly four years later, the originator of this anti-Trump spell crafted a new one to summon a "blue wave" in the 2020 presidential election to block Trump from re-election. This was cast on Halloween during a rare blue moon. A Facebook page dedicated to this purpose called "Bind Trump" had close to seven thousand supporters. The same year, the Los Angeles Times even published an article positively portraying the movement written by an individual who had joined in.[2] Witches claim the spell is a "binding" spell that does not cause harm. However, there are no real moral restraints in the practices of a witch, so what was stopping some of them from "spicing up" the spells as they were cast?

These dangerous activities of witches in society should not be seen as isolated events. The number of witches is not negligible and

---

[1] Seen and reported as witches on TikTok began posting about it and recruiting others to join #witchesforblm.

[2] *Los Angeles Times*, "Op-Ed: I put a spell on you, Mr. President," May 23, 2017.

their ability to negatively influence others and the world around them should not be underestimated.[3] Exorcist, Msgr. Rossetti, in a blog post on Oct. 30, 2021, stated, "One diocese estimated that there are more witches' covens in the diocese than Catholic institutions."[4] I heard the same thing from an additional exorcist. One priest I interviewed, Fr. Cyprian, who lives in a suburban area in the southeastern part of the US, said there were thirteen covens within the territory of one of the parishes where he served. It seemed that they attracted affluent people, which was the primary demographic in his parish. In one instance he recalled a Catholic builder, who was working on a local project, and to whom a coworker reported rumors that local witches were cursing him. Whenever he was approaching any sort of goal or deadline with his work, something would always go wrong, which he attributed to these reported curses.

Witch Stores

Another indicator of the growing presence of witchcraft is the establishment of witchcraft stores throughout the country. It is difficult to estimate the number, but it too is not negligible. There are many ways to find out if there are witch stores in your area or in an area to which you are traveling. The quickest way is to search using an online map with the keywords *metaphysical supply stores.* Then, zoom in to a city anywhere in the country and let the map populate the search results. Almost all of these will be witch stores of one kind or another. Only occasionally will a store with no connection to the occult be mentioned in the results, so always check the pictures, reviews, and website to verify.

As a sample, I searched a few random cities in the US and found the following results.[5] In Wichita, KS there were at least eleven occult stores and in Tucson, AZ there were at least seventeen. There were four in Casper, WY; five in Lansing, MI; and fifteen in Wilmington, NC. Margaret spoke about the destructive impact these

---

[3] While many reject the idea that the curses of witches have any effect on Christians, or on the majority of people in general, it remains true that individuals who are so dedicated to falsehood, superstition, and malevolent rituals will bring a corrosive effect upon society.

[4] Msgr. Rossetti blog, St. Michael Center for Spiritual Renewal, Exorcist Diary #162, "A Gathering of Witches."

[5] October 2022.

stores had on her family. Near their home, there was a witch store right down the road. Her children would often walk to the store, she said, knowing she did not approve. They bought stones and crystals and earth magic stuff. This occult influence undoubtedly played a powerful role in the downward spiral each child's life would eventually take. An acquaintance told me of a similar story, equally concerning for its potential impact. In her rural area, there is a small town with an occultic store in the main area of the town. On one occasion, while visiting the library, she heard the librarian talking openly to an associate about going to the occult store for crystals. This was within earshot of the children's section in the library. Clearly, parents need to be prepared to discuss these things with their children when they are at the appropriate age, or sooner if they are likely to hear about it even from their librarian.

Philomena commented, "Occult stores? Even tiny Bible-belt towns have occult stores…But no one stops it – Satan has rights in this country." These stores are not simply "novelty shops," as they are often billed. As Adelaide said, in one of the stores she frequented, she knew that the witches had "blessed" the items there in order to make them sell. Andrew agreed, stating that the frankincense and myrrh that he used in his rituals were purchased from a witch store. It is the same kind of incense that is used in the Church, he pointed out. He stressed, therefore, the importance of buying incense for home use from monastic communities and authentic Church suppliers.

Witch Markets

In addition to witch stores, there are also seasonal and periodic public festivities known as witch markets. For example, there is a monthly "Witches Market" in Austin, TX, established in 2015, at four different locations. One site advertising the event indicates it is recommended by "LGBTQ in Austin." The Facebook page for "Austin Witches Market," advertising all four locations, has a seventeen-second video clip advertising the event. What struck me was the music they incorporated into the clip, from the popular song

"Breakfast," by Dove Cameron.[6] This song, which called to my mind an image of the Hindu goddess Kali the destroyer, is apparently pretty popular with witches. It speaks, graphically, in lyrics and melody, about a feminine power which is a threatening and destructive force. This seems to appeal to witches, which should be alarming to us.

While researching for *The Rise of the Occult* and this present book, a social media acquaintance alerted me to an event just south of a major US town, in the middle of the country, called "Witches Night Out." It invites women only, twenty-one years old and older, to attend. They offer alcohol, the dark of night, mediums, tarot card readers, psychics, and a bunch of women dressed extravagantly like witches, in an area of the country in which there are at least forty witchcraft stores within sixty miles of the event.

---

[6] An American singer and actress who starred in roles in Disney children's shows from 2013-2021.

Chapter Four

Beliefs Within the Occult

It is not necessary for Christians to know all the things occultists do in the spiritual darkness of their practices. However, it is important for us to have a basic understanding of the sorts of things they embrace, and the sorts of beliefs they have, because we should regard the occult as a *false religion* whose members needs to be converted.[1] To convert the practitioners of a false religion to the Truth, it is necessary for us to understand what they currently believe. There are often some elements within a false religion, even witchcraft, which reflect a search for the Truth and which can be purified, transformed, or redirected for good by a conversion to the One True Faith.

There is no "system" to occult belief; it is as fractured and diverse as the lies the Evil One has uttered in order to draw these individuals into his malevolent society. This is most clearly seen in Wicca. Every Wiccan is his or her own authority, with their own spell book, their own preferences, their own choice of how and when and whether to follow the *Rule of Three* and the *Wiccan Rede*, their own choice of whether to curse or not, to believe in some deities or none, to believe in evil or not. Essentially, there is no overall theology or philosophy that governs the beliefs of this pagan religion.

"You are God"

With no need for an afterlife, Heaven, Hell, damnation, salvation, or a religious authority outside of oneself, the natural disposition of the occultist, New-Ager, magician, and Satanist is to

---

[1] It is a *real* religion in the sense that it has beliefs, practices, rituals, and a community of people who believe similarly. It is *false* in the sense that it is man-made and filled with errors.

believe that they themselves are God, or *a* god. "The New Age," Adam Blai said, "of course, is the Garden of Eden. It's essentially 'You can be God'." This emphasis on the person *as God* has manifested in the work of exorcists as well. Msgr. Rossetti observed that, on a number of occasions, demons have, from the mouths of afflicted souls, exclaimed, "I am God."[2] Former Yogi, Alex Frank said that, in Yoga, after you empty yourself of *self,* you are then supposed to realize that you are divine, that your *self* is actually God.

In Crowley's Thelema, which Andrew practiced, it was clear that self-worship was at the core. Outside of Thelema, in Wicca and other occult practices, there is the same focus, but people are simply unaware of it, Andrew said. In Thelema, self-worship was the highest virtue. It is essentially the exaltation of the personal will, even going so far as capitalizing the noun *will* when using it in this context. "Do what thou wilt shall be the whole of the law" is the essence of Thelema. A person's "True Will" is what is sought after: the power of expressing and manifesting *your Will* into reality.

Camilla said that within the widespread New Age promise of *spiritual healing* is, again, the proposal that we are gods. "We can attain perfection through spiritual striving if we follow a certain course or practice of meditation, exercises, and breathwork, and what they call *energy work*,"[3] she said. We can open up aspects of our personalities and souls and spirits to become enlightened and become like Christ ourselves. So," she continued, "in that paradigm, spiritual healing is discovering the 'god' within and letting the 'god' within heal us of the blocks that we have to realizing our own divinity. So, really, they define illness as a block to your own divinity."[4]

A big thing in the New Age, Gabriel said, is the belief that "you are special." Of course, this is another example of the inversion of the Truth. The New Age says that you are one of the "awakened" now. It is presented as a secret that only New-Agers know, and not

---

[2] Fr. Stephen Rossetti, *Diary of an American Exorcist* (Manchester: Sophia Institute Press, 2021), 103.

[3] For an explanation of this, see "Energy" later in this chapter.

[4] The truth is that we *can* attain spiritual perfection through cooperation with God's grace working through charity and prayer. The inversion of this truth is that it involves an *energy* instead of a gift from God and that it involves *discovering the god within* rather than receiving, from without, the grace of spiritual adoption and participation in the divine nature through Christ's Paschal Mystery and our incorporation into His Mystical Body, the Church.

accessible to people caught up in all of the formal religions. "This is the rabbit hole," Gabriel said again, adding, "There are many details to explain in order to understand in just what way you are special. They start talking about 'indigo children' if you are awake to this stuff. These are individuals whose souls were sent here from another planet in order to 'raise the vibration' of the earth. People with a 'low vibration' are angry people who have not been healed from their traumas. So, the goal is to raise everyone's vibration so we can all be one and accepting of others." This, Gabriel said, is supposed to enable everyone to reach "Christ consciousness." He added, "Christ consciousness has no belief in Jesus Himself. Jesus is just one of many spiritual masters, like Buddha and Gandhi. These have all 'unlocked' Christ consciousness and taught us to love everyone and be accepting of everything." The talk about being "special" goes so far as to tell New-Agers that they have "a mission" as a result of being awakened through the New Age. They have been "called" and "taught" but the question always remains: "By whom?"[5]

Though many people try to deny it, Philomena insists that the New Age is clearly part of the occult. Gabriel agreed, and said, "The New Age is hard to pin down; things are very subtle. Though it presents itself as the antidote to 'evil' [organized] religions, the New Age *is* a religion. It is a religion without any accountability," he said. "You don't feel bad about anything; you can be open and free; you don't feel bad about sin," he added. "The whole point is just to be accepting. It is pretty bizarre."

When Gabriel was practicing the New Age, he still believed that demons and darkness existed. He took note of Satanists messing with demons but thought that he was simply messing with "good spirits" and so he was okay. "I saw a separation between what they were doing and what I was doing," he said, but, admitting that he now sees that to be a lie, he added, "we were all doing the same ridiculous stuff."

---

[5] Here is another inversion of the Truth. Christians are *called* and given a certain *mission* by God. The New Age perverts this by saying this mission is to raise the vibration of the earth, become a *god* by your own efforts, and relativistically embrace all forms of moral expression.

Story: The Absurdity of the Occultic "I am God"

Margaret shared the following story which depicts how the absurdity of New Age teachings can be detected by a person who still has a mind focused on the search for Truth. When she was into New Age things in her early college years, she once had an appointment with a guru. In her mind at the time, she thought that if a priest were capable of instructing her in spiritual matters then this guru must *really* know the truth. She thought that since her mother and father were unenlightened about these things, she could forge a path and figure it out for everyone.

"Before going in," she remarked, "I looked up at the sky and said to God, 'Just lead me in Truth.' That was how I prefaced the meeting with the guru!" At this first meeting with the guru, he did not charge her but suggested that she go home and say a mantra in order to get prepared for the next meeting, which would be for a fee and more formal. "Is this really going to help?" she asked him. "Yes, this will help," he said. So, she went back home, to the downstairs den of her parents' house, where she was temporarily living after college. She took out the piece of paper upon which the guru had written the mantra and started repeating it. *I am God*, was all it said. She was supposed to say it over and over. "By the third time [of repeating it], I started laughing," she recalled. "This is a bunch of BS! No *way*! This is not Truth. And I never went back."

No Need for Satan

When an occultist becomes a god unto himself, there's no need for the figure of Satan in his spirituality. If Satan were within this belief system, he would feign submissiveness to the occultist. The demons[6] with whom occultists willingly communicate sometimes do present themselves as subordinate and obedient, but that is all a ruse that eventually erupts violently. And so many occultists actually believe *they*, and not the spirits, are the masters.

One witchcraft website said that Wiccans reject the idea of the devil because it is a construction of the Abrahamic religions, so, for

---

[6] These demons are regarded by occultists as powerful (and often dangerous) spirits but not as powerful or malicious as Satan is regarded in Christian theology.

this reason, they do not even consider him as a spirit able to be worshiped. John said that occultists, ceremonial magicians,[7] and pagans don't really believe in Satan; they see that belief as a Christian thing and most ceremonial magicians end up becoming Gnostics.[8] Most Wiccans and pagans also see the existence of Satan as simply a Christian teaching, he continued. They don't even think about it and never consider that deities like Loki, Hades, or Set, or other deities of the underworld, are different names for Satan. Therese said that, in Wiccan and witchcraft groups, occultists are expected to retrain their brains and not believe in Satan. Otherwise, they will be ridiculed for holding that belief and will be taught that they will be unable to grow or progress in these groups if they hold on to a Christian belief in Satan.

However, Wiccans and witches do have *dark gods* and *dark goddesses.* The use of the term "dark" here is not intended by Wiccans to convey the same image of evil and sin as Christians would intend by the term, but these entities are nonetheless demonic instigators of sin and licentiousness. John said occultists go their whole lives in the occult without seeing or thinking that Satan is behind any of it. John said that Satan hides in plain view but people just don't want to admit that they know he is there.

The Afterlife

"Everyone has their opinion," Therese explained. Some have a belief in an afterlife, some do not; some believe in a place called the *Summerland,* others are atheists; some believe their essence becomes one with, or absorbed into, the Universe, or simply integrated into the stars or the trees. Therese, who went from Wicca deep into magic, said, "They are not thinking of the afterlife; it's all about the *now*: what we need, are lacking, are angry about, what I am *owed*." Lucy, who went deep into the New Age, did not really have a belief about Hell, though she did think everyone, except the very worst of

---

[7] *Ceremonial* as a clarification that they are not *stage* magicians performing tricks.

[8] John said that almost every ceremonial magic order has a parallel "church" that is gnostic. These "churches" believe they have apostolic succession from Christ and can trace a priestly lineage through renegade French 19th-century gnostic priests who were also Catholic, or theosophical Anglican priests with valid succession from the time of Henry VIII.

25

the worst, went to some vaguely defined place called *Heaven*. She primarily believed in good and bad ghosts, good and bad magic, and good and bad witches. She did not regard herself to be in the "occult" but to be simply embracing *a belief* in the spiritual world. Andrew, as a Thelemite, personally believed in an afterlife, but not everyone who participates in the occult does. "In my experience," he said, "a lot of people seemed to believe in a type of Samsara (the cycle of life, death, and rebirth)." Andrew did not believe in damnation or salvation or in good or evil. "I only believed that there were those who actively pursued their True Will and those who did not."

Energy

Throughout the occult, there is a widespread belief in *energy*.[9] This is a very important point as it binds together all the spiritualities which fall under the umbrella of *the occult*. These energies are undefined cosmic or natural forces, as well as preternatural powers, many of which the occult practitioner can learn to summon, call upon, increase, and manipulate in order to bring about desired effects in the world, either for the practitioner himself or for (or against) another. These energies are believed to exist within us, the planet, the cosmos, and certain elements (like crystals, and some more than others). Energies are a focus of Yoga, the New Age, Wicca, witchcraft, Satanism, and Reiki, among others. It is practically a universal and unifying concept within the occult.

Wicca, for example, believes there are existing spiritual powers within nature that can be manipulated merely by the will of the individual. Nature, they say, has a mystical quality and we are tied to that quality on a spiritual level which enables our mere will, a spiritual faculty, to control those powers. Behind the Wiccan credal statement known as the *Law of Three*, or the *Threefold Law*, is a belief in energy. This *Law* states that "whatever you do to someone will come back to you threefold." This means whatever energy you send into the Universe will come back to you three times as powerful. As a result, Philomena explained, some people will not do "harmful spells," though, of course, as she pointed out, every spell is harmful since it is offensive to God. However, this "Law" is not a

---

[9] See chapters Five and Eight for more examples.

universal law among Wiccans, who are free to follow it or disregard it.

The witch, Lola, who is not a Wiccan but simply a witch, while describing the various practices that she embraced, also discussed the use of energy. She stated that witchcraft includes ancestor witchcraft, and work with angels, spirits, and demons, among others. She added, "We connect with energies and spiritual beings that a lot of people would simply pass off as fantasy." Lola added that witchcraft is largely based around energy and "intention." The ability to sense and to manipulate energy is the key. Witches are supposed to learn how to "pinpoint their energy, use it effectively, and draw energy from the earth so they don't deplete their own." This latter practice is apparently called *centering* or *grounding*. Wands are used by some witches to help raise their energy for spell work if they either have low energy, are producing low energy, or are not producing enough energy. Witches also use sage and crystals for this purpose. Crystals are believed to contain energy, and so, according to witches, need to be "cleansed" and "charged," and can increase energy for spell work.

Like other occult practices, Yoga also places an emphasis on energy. Yoga, as Alex Frank clarified, "is the training to isolate, control, and manipulate energy in your body in order to create more harmony between the mind and the body, so that you can ultimately be yoked to the Hindu Divine." Yoga trains the individual to be aware of his desires and emotions and separate these through meditation, enabling him to perceive the movement of energy in his body. "Chakra" is the term used to denote the energy points they focus on within the body. The goal in Yoga, as it is in magic, is to "manipulate this energy for your own gain, often for sexual ends," Alex said.

Reiki, which is a popular form of "energy work," is a prime example of the occult's reliance on energy. Camilla recounted the interesting story behind the creation of Reiki. It began with a Japanese doctor, Mikao Usui, who wanted to understand how Jesus and the Buddha were able to perform healings. Apparently, he located some secret magical texts and then himself was able to "heal" a lot of people. However, after three years, they were no longer healed. He concluded that the people did not pay him enough money for the healings and that is why their ailments returned. He then

27

developed a system where people paid money and the Reiki practitioners who performed these "healings" were able to receive "initiations" into higher and higher realms of energy and consciousness, enabling them to channel more energy.[10] Adam Blai explained that Reiki leads the practitioner into a state of idolatry, since the practitioner is proclaiming, "I am the healing force, not God." In the US, he added, there are only three levels of Reiki that are given to practitioners. In Japan, there are five. In levels 4 and 5, the teaching is much more explicit which states that there is a *familiar spirit* at work when a practitioner is doing the rituals. The truth, then, he explained, is that a spirit is doing these things, not you, but they don't tell people this in the lower levels.[11]

Satanism, likewise, as depicted in the documentary by Ciaran Lyons, believes there are energies that the Satanist can summon, which can be manipulated and used to manifest changes in the material world. Even those Satanic groups that "don't believe in the preternatural or supernatural" nonetheless believe in energies and forces of darkness, which are immense and can be channeled and charged internally. These forces are then empowering to the individual, allowing him to manifest changes in the world, all done through their rituals, which they continue to claim are merely "psychodrama."

Chaos Magic

John explained that today, in part due to the internet, "everybody does everything." Each form of witchcraft and the occult is borrowing from the others, invoking demons from occult traditions that are not strictly what they are practicing. This, he said, is called *chaos magic.* A Wiccan, for example, who is regarded to be on the *right-hand path*, since they try to label their rituals as "good

---

[10] A similar explanation states that it was a student of the Mikao Usui's successor who discerned the need for payment. This student, Hawayo Takata, also brought Reiki to the U.S. Takata is the one who saw that those who paid money for the healing, and "perceived the value" of it, were the ones who were healed. (Catholic World Report, "A Disturbing Substitute for Faith," April 18, 2011). The "International Center for Reiki Training" disputes the necessity for charging a fee for Reiki, but not the history of the practice.
[11] Blai video.

magic," are now often calling upon *goetic* demons,[12] which are traditionally from the darker *left-hand path* of magic. He sees this increase in calling upon demons as a sign that demons have become bolder today. A few exorcists have commented in agreement on this point. In the past, John explained, magicians used to go through rituals and make specific forms of progress before they encountered and worked directly with demons. Today, however, demons are showing up at rap concerts[13] and are getting witches to think they are their friends and that these structures are not necessary.

Chaos magic originated in England in the 1960s in an attempt, led by a prominent occultist, to do away with the ceremonial rituals and to seek whatever form of magic suffices for that which is sought by the individual. Chaos magicians take from every culture and are no longer systematic in their approach. Occultists of this form are not bound to a certain tradition but embrace everything, as well as rejecting any borders or structures to their practice.

Deities

In the occult, the practitioner very often seeks to interact with spirits. Many occultists know exactly what they are doing, explicitly invoking demons, while others remain deceived, believing they are interacting with various deities from a variety of ancient cultural pantheons. As John explained, pagans believe they are petitioning deities, or the "old gods," and do not regard these rituals as *spells*. Celtics and Druids and Egyptians do, but Greco-Roman and Norse see them as *prayers* instead. As a result, practitioners of the latter two engage in praying to a specific deity for health and wealth and other things.

Within witchcraft, whether of the *left* or the *right*, Satanic or independent, invocations are oriented toward spirits. They do not

---

[12] These demons are taken from a compendium from the Middle Ages and the Renaissance time period, which collected the names of all the demons with which ceremonial magicians traditionally worked.

[13] The now infamous rap concert by Travis Scott on November 5, 2021, which presented itself as a portal to another world and was filled with occultic images. During the concert, eight people were crushed and killed, and two died later in the hospital. Concertgoers were oppressed by a spirit of panic and later went to social media to describe the event as feeling "like being in Hell." Many of the occultists I interviewed referred to this concert as an occult ritual.

pray to deities but *invoke* spirits to assist them. Thus, they incorporate spiritism, and these spirits feign being spirits of the dead ("necromantic"), leading the practitioners to believe they are getting their ancestors and other dead people to assist them.

Within ceremonial magic, John explained, there are many things happening, in what is called an *inner order* and an *outer order*. On one side, the outer order work, the occultist is developing his own psychic powers, creating the wealth and knowledge that he seeks by developing, for example, the power to acquire the wealth or the systems of memory he desires. This involves self-development, psychic abilities, and habits and skills of a societal, psychological and physical nature. On the other side, the inner order work, he is working with things like the pure elements, earth, air, fire, water, ether, as well as with both the good angels, so he claims, and the fallen angels, referred to as the *goetic* demons.

One website that focused on Wicca and witchcraft teachings and rituals said Wiccans may also pray to various deities, some from the Greek, Egyptian, Roman, or Celtic pantheon, as well as Mother Earth or a combination Mother/Father, also known as *the Lord and the Lady*. They also rely on spirit guides, something in the New Age movement, though they claim the New Age is very different and based on esoteric knowledge whereas Wicca is nature-based. In their rituals, they evoke, i.e., *summon*, entities in their rituals and spells, as well as channel their own magical energies. Resembling ceremonial magic, they use magic both for inner and outer work, work devoted to personal growth and work devoted to interaction with deities.

In Dianic circles of Wicca,[14] there are elaborate chants and music, calling upon Diana to appear to the practitioner, praising her beauty and greatness, and placing their trust in her help.[15] Helena explained how they would worship one of the goddesses, either Diana or another called Morrigan. The meeting of the coven entailed simple socializing as people gathered. Then, they would go into meditation and "trance work" to "meet the goddess," at which point they would receive the messages she wanted to communicate. After encountering the goddess, she said, "The area would be purified with

---

[14] Often referred to as Dianic Witchcraft.
[15] Spells8. "Diana, Goddess of the Hunt and the Moon [Wiccan Worship Song]." *YouTube*, July 20, 2019, youtube.com/watch?v=YqblVmRbVVE.

sage and then each of us would purify each other with sage." They also used an altar which was decorated with statues and candles and anything related to the specific ritual performed. A head priestess led the group and they all gathered around the altar. Members of the coven would rotate calling upon the cardinal directions and the elements of the earth to protect them.[16] They would then evoke the goddess, or multiple deities, depending on the spells they intended to cast. They would use oils, incense, song, dance, and "work themselves up into a frenzy, creating energy, a 'cone of power'," she said. When the priestess determined that the energy had "reached its peak," they would "release it to the universe and to whatever the goal was for that meeting."

Interacting with "Deities"

Helena explained that they would receive answers from the "goddess" through guided meditation and astral projection. "You looked a lot at what you considered 'signs' in your life," she said. John, who worked with demons directly, said that demons would communicate psychologically, i.e., mind to mind. "They produce mental phenomena accompanied by manifestations in the physical realm. You become attuned to things and notice them," he added, "concluding, for example, that a specific deity is speaking to you through the events. You will notice synchronicities happening. This communication comes through each individual person's psychology since demons are spirits and speak through the intellectual powers."[17]

When an occultist is seeking a direct message for something personal, some will use such techniques as a Ouija board or scrying,[18] John said. Sometimes, they will hear a voice in their head,

---

[16] When I asked her if they purified the area because there was some sort of evil or danger, she told me that, yes, the goddess could absolutely be dangerous. This is explained more in *The Rise of the Occult*, page 173.

[17] To a Christian, this can appear to resemble how Our Lord and the Communion of Saints interact with us. However, the issue here is that occultists are communicating with false gods and demons, which is gravely sinful and extremely dangerous. Though it is sinful, it does not prevent these demons from responding. This is a mockery of Divine Providence and prayer. It also proves the point of the great Saints that we must carefully discern spiritual manifestations and learn that God works in a way contrary to how the devil works.

[18] Seeking messages or visions through a medium like a crystal ball or other device.

like a direct communication. The spirits' technique is to allow you to encounter what you really want to encounter; not everything but only enough to encourage you to continue going deeper. They provide a lot of synchronicities to keep you going but without completely answering your questions. It is like the carrot as bait before the horse, to draw you further in.

Adelaide said that when she was using tarot cards, demons would communicate with her, not with a voice but with more of a nudge. She would then share with her group what she was receiving. She described it like this: "I would be talking before formulating a thought. The words were coming without my thinking them, and I was always accurate. But I was not possessed." Fr. Sebastian said demonic communication is telepathic and only in the mind, in a way that the person knows it is not their own thoughts.

In some forms of the occult, such as Palo, an entity will also possess or "ride" a person and use them as a mouthpiece and go around and give answers and direct messages to the entity's "children," who must obey what is told to them by the entity, since it was directed right to them. As can be imagined, there are lots of human abuses that occur as a result of a belief in this sort of power.

In her interview with Bob Larson, Zeena Schreck explained that she had personal experiences of Set, the Egyptian deity she worshipped at the time (1997), in her own rituals and also within groups. Set spoke to them in various ways, not all of which they understood. "Telepathic" is one way to describe the experience, which Zeena described as "powerful." Nikolas Schreck, her husband at the time, stated, "We feel that the presence of the prince of darkness [a description of Set] is a part of us. He speaks to us through many means." "Empowered" is an accurate way to refer to the fruits of the encounter, they said. Zeena also explained that Set was living inside of them and that they represented him.[19]

---

[19] Satania. "Showdown with Satanism - Bob Larson Interviews Zeena Lavey and Nikolas Schreck." *YouTube*, 14 March 2020. youtube.com/watch?v=jfk9NZ5pgRw; Larson video #2.

Deities as Friends

Though it might not be a universal distinction, the witch Lola and Zeena both avoided the term "worship" in reference to the deity, opting instead for the term "follow." Zeena strongly rejected the idea of being possessed by Set, even though she said he was living inside of them. They said that they remained in control of their own spirits despite their affiliation with him.[20]

On one witchcraft forum, there was a discussion of the sadness of having a deity leave you. Apparently, some witches experience the "real" presence of, among others, Greek gods and goddesses. At times, these entities will "leave" and go do work somewhere else. One individual in the discussion, for example, said that the two deities, Aphrodite and Apollo, informed her that they would soon be leaving. Three other gods, Hades, Persephone, and Selene, however, told her they would remain with her and comfort her in her resulting grief. In their interview with Bob Larson, Larson pressed Zeena and Nikolas on whether they fraternize with *demons*. Nikolas eventually responded, "As black magicians, we look upon the powers of darkness as our friends, as peers; we do not worship them; they don't control us." Zeena added, "Nor do we view them as particularly interested with our outcomes, as your Jehovah would be."[21]

This statement from Zeena and Nikolas is reminiscent of a story told by the exorcist Fr. Matthew about a man he visited at the request of the man's family. The family had long been worried about him and his occult practices, and they wanted Father to simply reach out to him and see if he would be willing to give up his association with demonic spirits. In the course of the conversation, the man told Fr. Matthew, "The demons are my friends; I don't want to be separated from them. I am looking forward to spending eternity with them in Hell."

Deities as Demons

Andrew said that, while there are many out there who are convinced they are contacting and working with "gods and

---

[20] Larson video #2.
[21] Ibid.

goddesses," there are others, like himself, who knew with full knowledge that they were working with demons and directly summoning or calling upon them.[22] Explaining the difference between magic and Wicca, Andrew said, "A lot of people who are into Wicca, they're not doing what I was doing. I knew I was working with demons, knew it was dangerous. I did not believe in Heaven or Hell; it was a different cosmology. People in Wicca, they don't believe they're doing anything wrong. They believe they are in harmony with nature, doing a pre-Christian naturalistic worship. They think they have their own divine image that the earth gives them. It is the same for the New Age, interlocked today with Wicca. These crystal shops and the like, it is New Age with a Wiccan flavor."

Demons as Friends

Fr. Anselm said that many problems emerge from a lack of good teaching on the devil. People become afraid of the devil in the absence of the teaching that it is actually the devil who is afraid of *us* when we love God and remain in a state of grace. As surprising as it may seem, people also become inclined to think of the devil and the demons as friends, not realizing that, if we call upon them or seek their assistance, we risk placing ourselves in a state of mortal sin and losing the protection of Almighty God. Former New-Ager Angela Ucci stated, in an interview with Michael Knowles, that this is in fact a belief in the New Age, one which she held and taught to others. She said they are taught to "integrate your inner demons" and "make friends with your demons because they are teaching you something." This, she said, is all "under the guise that Satan is liberating." This friendship with demons lowers your guard against them in general, a misunderstanding that is very dangerous. Fr. Anselm explained, "There are many shows that depict the devil in this way, and it points to part of the problem when we stop teaching about the devil and the danger of evil."

---

[22] "Evoking" and "invoking."

Chapter Five

Spells and Rituals

Since there is no authority overseeing the religious practices within Wicca, witchcraft, Satanism, and other forms of the occult which utilize spells and rituals, these practices will vary in name and number and kind. However, it does seem that some specific spells are common to practitioners of both Wicca and witchcraft, and those Satanists who embrace the latter. A basic understanding of what occultists are seeking is helpful for those who are trying to reach out to them and educate them on the emptiness, and the danger, of seeking these things through superstitious occult rituals.

Banishing spells are used to remove a negative thing or person from a person's life, such as by making the person stop seeing them or thinking about them. *Sweetening* spells are intended to make someone think well of you, or help you with legal issues, jobs, and relationships. *Binding* spells are intended to restrict something or someone from harming themselves or others. According to one site, it is not advisable to use binding spells against people but witches can use it against themselves to stop a bad habit. However, given the well-publicized cursing and "binding" of President Trump, it is apparent that witches do use it against people.[1] *Freezing* spells are used to silence someone, particularly their words or actions. In addition to these, there are spells used to ward off negative energies, to help them move forward with a situation or decision, to remove a hex or a cause of illness or misfortune, to protect and give health to animals (pets), to transfer the energies of the moon to their homes and possessions, to draw positive energy that will "manifest" success, to return intended harm back to the one who sent it, to get worldly success (such as through "bay leaf magic"), to acquire better finances

---

[1] Binding spells are often what amounts to a "curse" for a witch.

through the moon's power, and to pass tests through sun spells, among many others.

A specific form of protection spell that Christopher spoke about is called a "ward." "Wards," he said, "to protect one's home, car, or person are by far the most common and unnoticed spells." The wording used for wards varies depending on the kind of occult group at issue. Incense is utilized by almost all occultic groups for these ward spells. Helena said that her spells would focus on protection for her home, binding people so they can't harm her, attaining certain goals (some small, like a parking space, and others more important, like a job or new car), and casting a circle of protection in order to raise her energy. "There is a spell for everything," she said adding, from her personal experience, "The most commonly used spells are related to goals."

Occultic "sacramentals"

Along with spells, witchcraft (and many other forms of the occult) makes use of common items in order to do their occultic work. Many of these items will sound familiar to Christians, but this must not cause us alarm. As exorcists have emphasized, the fact that the occult has rituals and uses elements that are similar to what the Church uses does not invalidate the religious use of rituals and ritual items; most importantly, it does not justify ending the use of rituals in the Church. On the contrary, it reveals two things: that the occult seeks to mock the Church and to present an enticing counterfeit of the One True Faith, and that people naturally seek ritual. If they do not turn to God and His Holy Church for the rituals which have His blessing within them, and which have their origin in His inspiration, they will often turn to the counterfeit which, by the devil's activity, promises to bring real-world effects.

The ritual items used by the occult include altars, candles, incense, water, salt, oils, and bells, among others. Bells, for example, are used by witches in their practice with the belief that they will ward off negativity in the home. Bells are believed to also guard doors in the home and bring positive energy, protection, and prosperity. One witch website advised the use of salt as an "elemental protection agent," sprinkling it on the floor in the home to cleanse the energies. Wiccans also utilize crystals for purposes similar to spells. Tarot cards are used for divination and, in his experience, Christopher said the most common rituals he saw were tarot cards and runes, as divination tools, but not Ouija boards. The use of tarot card readings was regarded as an effective way "to get a sense of someone or a particular path forward, especially in relationships." Andrew added that, in addition to what he called "folk magick," there is the use of talismans and effigies, which, he said, are "magickly 'programmed' to achieve various effects, usually seeking protection or healing." Lucy used incense in her rituals, which seemed to be a common practice. Lucy said that the incense she used was supposed to "clear the air and increase your psychic ability...help you connect with spirits and be able to tune into the messages easier."

In Christianity, the moon is an image of Our Lady, the celestial light that reflects the light of the sun. In witchcraft, the moon is a powerful figure which reveals yet another attempt of the devil to invert the Truth. "The moon," Helena said, "is very connected to the goddess; it is part of her essence." Helena's coven would leave out items, such as candles, crystals, and jars of water, at night under the full moon. "They could then be used in various rituals," she said, "as they are considered now more powerful." Their main rituals were always held at night and at the full moon as a result of this belief. A witchcraft website spoke about a "moon water spell." This is found in various grimoires.[2] It involves leaving a cup of water out under the moonlight, even on cloudy days. The witch then "consecrates" it by thanking the moon for this sacred water. Moon water enables the witch to harness the power of the element of water and of the moon in the witch's ritual practice. As a result of its exposure to moonlight, they believe it is charged with a "magical intention." Water "charged" under the moon is believed to take on different magical properties depending on which phase the moon was in during that ritual. Highlighting the superstitious and irrational quality of such rituals, witches are warned to be sure not to leave the moon water out too long lest it come in contact with sunlight.[3]

---

[2] Grimoires are occultic books of spells.
[3] See *The Rise of the Occult*, p 173, for certain dangers that may appear in the process of harvesting this moon water.

The Purpose of Spells

The witch Lola spoke in a dismissive way of the popular and Hollywood concepts of witchcraft as possessing a truly "magical" power that can enable the practitioner to do extraordinary things. She described witchcraft as an assistant to life, "not a fix for all worldly problems" nor a power "to create things out of nothing or fly around or turn people into animals." Some witches consider using spells to win the lottery.[4] Lola discouraged such a practice. She said, "Don't cast a spell to win the lottery; it is not going to work. You have to be realistic. The chances of winning are already so small that even the small boost that the spell will provide, it still won't manifest for you. You have to put in real hard work along with the magic." Essentially, she said, life can be *improved* through witchcraft. She listed some of the benefits of witchcraft as: "Find new love and work, protect yourself from psychic attacks, realize new potentials, find new money when struggling, boost self-confidence and control in an out-of-control world." She said a witch can use it to help herself and others and "bring a sense of spiritual stability to your life." Regarding the more extraordinary spiritual things, she stated that witchcraft is "a link" to new things. By utilizing divination, the witch can see "the potential future."[5] Through "astral projection," the witch can "travel through planes of existence and connect with spiritual beings you have never connected with before." She said this includes connecting to other spirits like "dragon energies, elementals, spirits, and even fairies."

What happens, and what is desired, in the rituals of different occultic practices will vary. However, there is a unity of intention in these practices, since magicians, Wiccans, witches, and Satanists all accept Crowley's definition of magic as "the art and science of changing reality to conform with the will." This belief was held, for example, by both John, when he was a ceremonial magician, as well as by a website dedicated to teaching about Wicca and witchcraft. Therefore, although the ceremonials they embraced in the process

---

[4] See *The Rise of the Occult*, 211, for Andrew's story about casting a spell to win the lottery.

[5] This admission is interesting since the diabolical, which is the agency the witch is ultimately utilizing, can only see the "potential" future as well. Demons can, of course, be very accurate due to the immensity of their knowledge of the present and their ability to guess the future based on this information.

may vary, the intention is the same in the end. Further, though some spiritual seekers will turn away from the occult once they learn that these occult practices are not authentic ancient religions but simply modern concoctions, the arbitrary rituals of the occult still possess a dangerous power. The fact that witches act like witches is a danger in itself, whether it is a "real" pagan ritual or not. All pagan rituals are contrived by fallen man under the inspiration of demons and are dangerous as a result of this diabolical association, be they ancient or modern.

A Day in the Life of an Occultist

As a Thelemite, following the way of Aleister Crowley, Andrew's day was filled with rituals, including Yoga breathing techniques and postures; worship of the sun at sunrise, noon, sunset, as well as midnight;[6] what is known as the Lesser Banishing Ritual of the Pentagram (LBRP), reading tarot cards, and the daily recitation of the 'Gnostic Creed'." He also studied astrology, practiced scrying,[7] used talking boards (Ouija), and had a black mirror to summon spirits. He used incense, makeshift vestments, and chant in his rituals. These rituals involved formal prescribed actions and there were rubrics that he more or less followed. Some people, he said, do their rituals on a whim, like with a Ouija board, but his main practice was ceremonial.

As Andrew described it, "Even the most mundane task had to be transfixed on ascertaining my *True Will* – answering the questions: Who am I? Why am I here? And how do I live it out every day without ever diverting myself from that path? That's what it was about, and that's why I took it very seriously. To me," he made clear, "it was a religion. I woke up with the sun, I did these things at noon, at sunset, and again at midnight. Once you have the discipline to do this consistently for months, you then add things – it's almost like a workout routine."

"For most practitioners," Helena said, "your witchcraft was incorporated into every aspect of your life." It is through the practice of this craft that witches believe they are connected to the goddess

---

[6] "Basically," Andrew added, "the same moments throughout the day that Catholics would pray the Angelus."

[7] Seeking to know the future through a medium such as a crystal ball.

and to the earth, increase their power and abilities, and obtain the goddess' protection. In a given day, she would say morning prayers to the goddess, add cinnamon to her morning coffee to obtain wealth, sweep her kitchen with a witch's broom, cast spells of protection and harmony, meditate at her altar, talk to plants[8] and the elements, among other things. "Literally, every part of my day," she said, "could easily be tied to witchcraft. It was something to strive for." Helena said that her rituals in witchcraft would all have a specific focus, such as protection for a person, cursing someone, or a particular desire for the coven, among other things. There would also be times where she was simply worshipping the goddess.

---

[8] She is an herbalist and, now that she has converted, she said, "The thanks now go to God, not to the plant!"

Chapter Six

Story: The Dangers of Witchcraft – Spirits in a Witch's Home

In my ongoing research for this book and for *The Rise of the Occult*, I listened to several active witches explain their beliefs on various topics. While I do not recommend this for most people, it was very informative and confirmed what I was learning from the former occultists whom I was interviewing. Further, it provided examples of the dangers that occultists fall into and the blindness that prevents them from realizing what is happening to them. Among these dangers is what one online witch called "spirit encounters." Her story exemplified an important warning which can serve as a lesson for those who think dabbling in witchcraft is "just for fun" and for those who think there is nothing to be afraid of when practicing witchcraft. Further, this story is important for priests to hear: some witches are fleeing witchcraft because they are opening up doors to the demonic that they never knew were possible and, as a result, are suffering diabolical attacks which might push them to the Church for help. Exorcists have spoken about the rise in the number of such cases. The witch featured here is present in our world today, and she is just one of *many* who are practicing and proclaiming the ways of witchcraft to an ever more gullible population of paganized people.

Here is her story:

In discussing various topics with her audience, Lola turned to the issue of "ghosts" or, as she clarified, "strange spirit encounters." She explained, "I'm definitely finding more and more that I am getting strange spirit encounters time and time again." She then explained that her house is "fairly well protected" by means of the rituals she has done, including "home protections, wards, and shields." "I like to keep my space fairly insulated from external

41

interactions, just so that I can have a nice, safe, calm environment," she said.

The new "spirit encounters" she has been experiencing are "quite unusual," she stated, and she wasn't sure exactly why they were happening. "It is getting a little bit strange over here," she said. Importantly, she admitted that she *doesn't understand* these manifestations, adding, "I can't tell entirely what's causing this." Despite that, while giving the impression of being concerned, she was not *overly* concerned.

Naïvely, as she has "protected" her house by her rituals, she has also instituted "rules" in her house regarding spirits' coming and going. She said, "Here, spirits are allowed to pass into my space as long as they come with some kind of warning message, or they are there peacefully. I don't typically allow anything into my space that is negative or aggressive." She presumed to have the power to control spirits but stated at the same time, regarding the new manifestations, "All of the spirit encounters that I've had recently have been for a reason. I just can't quite figure out what that is yet."

The manifestations, as I am calling them, are, unfortunately for her, just that – likely signs of a diabolical presence. "I have had whispering; I usually don't have whispering in my house," she said. Her admissions reveal that she has clearly, at some point in the past, already invited spirits into her home. She explained, "None of the present spirits, or should I say the *consistent* spirits, have a whispery tendency. You'll often find that some spirits will prefer to interact in certain ways and none of the spirits that are permanent residents in my home have a whispery tendency." In addition, she heard "phantom noises in places where there shouldn't be noises." She has also seen a lot of "small shadows appearing."[1] These are things that, apparently, she has not had in her house before. She stated that she did experience this in a previous home, some years ago, but this is the first time it has happened in her current home.

The most significant event, which was actually "unsettling" to her, occurred when she heard the sound of knocking on cabinets and appliances in her kitchen. The sound progressed from the back of the kitchen all the way to the door that was right next to where she was

---

[1] See Fraune, *Slaying Dragons*, 19, for a presentation on how demons can manifest as shadowy figures.

sitting, getting louder and louder as it came closer. Her reaction to this kitchen banging was to simply ignore it and hope it went away. Prior to this encounter, her experiences with spirits ranged from those that simply wanted to communicate with her to those on the negative side that wanted to "mess" with her. The latter is the kind that she had also decided to ignore, thinking they would realize she was not interested and get bored and leave. In the past, when she had tried to tell a difficult spirit to *stop*, it had often made things worse.

She was <u>very confident</u> that the other witches, from her nearly two hundred *thousand* YouTube subscribers, who actively follow her standard witchcraft content, "will likely have experienced this." This encounter mentioned above, involving the unsettling banging in the kitchen, took place between the modern pagan witch festivals of Beltane and Litha, during the months of May and June. This, like Samhain, she believes, is a time where spirits' activity is on the rise. She said, "This is definitely a time in the year where you will likely start noticing spirit encounters really increasing dramatically."

There are numerous *red flags* in this account. Lola is already immersed in serious sins because of her embrace of the superstitious beliefs and practices which she detailed in this account. Thus, she is not protected by grace and is vulnerable to extraordinary diabolical influence. Further, she has already explicitly invited numerous nameless spirits into her home and, by establishing rules for their activity, has deepened her level of consent to their presence and activity. Given her spiritual state, a soul from Purgatory would not visit her since she, being absent of grace, cannot offer any spiritual assistance from which such a soul would benefit. Thus, particularly given the presence of "small shadows appearing" and of a sinister banging in the kitchen, what she is most likely dealing with is a demon. If this witch is not careful, and does not cease these dabblings, she will soon need an exorcist, if not already. Given that this is apparently a common experience for witches like her, those who have loved ones in the occult, and those who are helping witches leave the occult, should take note of this concrete danger they are likely facing.

Chapter Seven

The Dark Side in the Occult: Subjective Morality and Cursing

One of the inherent and universal dangers of the occult is the fact that it is characterized by a total moral subjectivism. The occultist, whether a witch, a Wiccan, a New-Ager, a magician, or a Satanist, does not view himself as being bound by any moral code or creed or religious authority. Wicca comes the closest with the *Rule of Three* and the *Wiccan Rede*, but there is nothing binding the Wiccan to the observance of such "rules," leading many of them to turn away from this arbitrary constriction on their "spiritual freedom" whenever it suits them. As a result, those who walk down the spiritual path of the occult truly do enter upon the dark side of religion.

Regarding the *Wiccan Rede*, Wiccan websites often state that Wiccans are supposed to abide by this restriction, which amounts to "a rule of conduct which prohibits Wiccans from harming others." "Rede" is an archaic English word that means "advice" and is not actually a rule or prohibition, but "rather a word of guidance." Further, one Wiccan website revealingly stated, *"there are many possible interpretations and no ultimate meaning"* to the *Wiccan Rede*. Adam Blai addressed this as well, saying, "There is no *one* Wicca; there is no *one* witchcraft, there is no *one* book like we have a Bible." While it started with Gardner's loose vision, there are now millions of versions of Wicca and witchcraft.[1]

Generic paganism[2] is also plagued by subjective morality. While morality was in Timothy's mind as an important issue, especially as a father to girls in our perverted culture, being raised as a pagan himself left him with no framework to understand morality. The

---

[1] Blai video.
[2] Celtic, Druid, Greek, Egyptian, Norse, Native American, etc.; generally called *neo-pagan*. Timothy was raised by a mother who followed a Native American religion.

pagan community did not provide a unifying moral structure or moral compass. He was left to figure it out for himself once he got married. Timothy saw that the pagan community did not offer a good solution to this dilemma. It was also difficult to develop a good strong connection to any truth within paganism because the community was too diverse. As one example, there were no specific teachings on sexual morality; what he and his wife did see presented there was not in harmony with the morality his family had developed for themselves. The pagan community, he said, defines itself much like the Protestant world does. As Protestantism is essentially "not Catholic," so the pagan community tended to define itself a lot as "not Christian"; but it provided no moral system of its own. As a result, Timothy said, "It is going to embrace immorality because, simply put, that is human nature."

John said that, in Wicca, Thelema, Freemasonry, and others, permissiveness is the game, and this is clearly seen in the teachings they present to their followers. The Wiccan poem *Charge of the Goddess* contains the line, "All acts of love and pleasure are My rituals." This poem was written by Gerald Gardner, compiled from the writings of Charles Leland and Aleister Crowley. Doreen Valiente eventually rewrote it in prose form, which is now the best-known version. Aleister Crowley, from whom Thelema originated, proclaimed "Love under will," that is, your *own* will, according to your *own* preferences. Freemasonry, another occultic organization, which pivots around the embrace of a religious syncretism, requires its members to adhere to a tolerance of all religions. Thus, throughout the occult, all things are permitted.[3]

Prevalence of Cursing

Naturally flowing from this permissiveness and adoration of one's own will and desires is the tendency toward malice. Our fallen human natures, when completely loosed from the guidance of God's Law and inspirations, will be inflamed by our many disordered passions. Malice, expressed through the occult in the form of

---

[3] John also pointed out that the spirit of permissiveness is prevalent throughout the Church today. This pairs suspiciously with accusations, as well as clear evidence, of occultic practices among some members of the hierarchy.

cursing, is just one of those. Christians must remember that any power of the Enemy is subordinate to God's permissive will. The demons are not free to do whatever they would like and the rituals of the occult have no intrinsic power. Christians especially, protected as they are when in a state of grace, by the grace and Precious Blood of Our Lord Jesus Christ, do not need to fear the curses and hexes of witches and Satanists. The greatest danger posed by curses is for the ones who cast them.

The use of cursing varies quite a bit among modern occultists. Based on his five years of experience as a Thelemite, Andrew said, "I only ever met a handful of witches and Wiccans willing to participate in curses, and I never really saw them as being mentally sound, to be quite honest." Helena, as a former Wiccan, said that, while a Wiccan could theoretically curse anything, she rarely did, preferring, as was their custom, to issue a binding spell instead. One time, however, motivated by anger, she did issue a curse against a home. "In Dianic Wiccan covens," she added, "there was a great emphasis on cursing men that had hurt women or children in one form or another." They believed that curses could be used to take away someone's power or to let harm come to them.

From Therese's perspective, while new Wiccans typically refuse to cast curses, saying, "No, no, no! We don't want *that*!", eventually, she said, as morality becomes relative, your mind begins to say, "If it benefits me, then it doesn't matter." Everything eventually becomes utilitarian. Therese herself followed this path and was eventually getting paid by people to cast spells that would, for example, split up relationships and drive a person toward her client instead. She did spells for those people and admitted, "There was a lot of cursing."

In the occult, from Philomena's perspective, it is not the case that "everyone curses everything." However, there are some awful people in the occult who will take that approach, such as going through stores and cursing random things. Philomena has also seen occult practitioners randomly curse a home as they pass by. They do this simply because they feel they *can* and the exercise of this "power" is intoxicating. A curse has a malicious intent within it and this "ability" to harm people contributes to the occultists' sense of power. While none of it is benign, occultists' *willingness* to do this indicates there is a significant demonic influence over them.

When someone is issuing curses, Philomena said, "It is like firing a loaded gun into a crowd: you're gonna hit someone but you don't really care." Andrew said he only engaged in curses a few times and was never sure they worked. Others, though, claimed they were successful, but Andrew had no way of confirming their success. Regarding the prevalence of curses, he said, "I will say, in retrospect, that I do absolutely believe that some occultists most certainly deliberately curse objects." Though he is certain that there are individuals who curse random objects wherever they go in their day, Andrew said he has never met any.

John, who has a rather vast occult experience, distinguished curses from spells. Through curses an occultist would seek to bring about harm by taking something away from the target: to get someone sick, to have someone lose their job, lose fame or power, lose love, or lose knowledge. Spells, sometimes called "blessings," are the opposite, seeking to impart these same things to people: health, money, prestige, power, love, and knowledge.

A Witch's Perspective on Cursing

In addition to the great divergence in practice, there are also rather intense disagreements about cursing in the witchcraft world. The witch Lola said that she often finds these disagreements in the online witch community. She herself has absolutely no problem with curses. She admitted that it is a difficult subject in witchcraft chat rooms, but she blamed a lot of the problems on a failure to properly distinguish between, and on an improper conflation of, "Wicca" and "witchcraft."

In one video, Lola referred to curses as "negative workings against someone." These included a "hex, jinx, or cross." Wiccans and witches often hesitate at the idea of cursing because they think they are bound by the *Rule of Three*, as well as the *Wiccan Rede*, but Lola clarified this, stating, "The confusion between Wicca and witchcraft makes people think that it is wrong to curse because it goes against the *Rule of Three*, the *Wiccan Rede*, etc., but witchcraft is not Wicca." The *Rede*, she said, came later than witchcraft, which has no such prohibitions. "The confusion," she said, "that 'you cannot curse,' [is] because people are conflating Wicca and witchcraft and the *Rede* says don't curse/harm."

Lola said there are many people who genuinely believe that a person should take the approach of "kill them with kindness" instead of cursing. She sees this all over the comment sections of the online witch community.[4] Yes, she said, this could work, so it should be considered before engaging in cursing. "However," she added, "I don't believe that you should desperately try to find some miraculous alternative if, genuinely, the best way to go about fixing this problem is to just *get it over with*: curse, hex, jinx, cross, whatever it may be."

When Lola hears people speaking adamantly about how "love and light can cure the world," she agreed that it is indeed good to be kind and gentle, but, she said, "That doesn't get stuff done." She continued, "Sometimes, you genuinely do just need to 'get on with it' and do some negative work, or some *return to sender* work, or something to send that energy back that way, or to send it their way in the first place if they really need a lesson." Lola then added an interesting observation about modern Wiccans. Today, she has seen an attitude becoming more common, which she described as, "Do no harm but take no ___."[5] This comment made me wonder if this is due to the growing belief among Wiccans that they *are* capable, supposedly, by their veiled fraternizing with demons, of tapping into these dark powers and, they may then believe, to actually send curses against others. If they believe it works, and there is no morality stopping them, why would they hesitate to engage in the practice?

As Lola addressed the issue, her permissiveness toward cursing was clearly based upon a foundation of moral relativism. She said, "It is all down to your personal morals. Everyone's moral spectrum is different. A lot of people push their own morality onto others within the community." She added, "Our morality is our morality. It is our spectrum that is defined by our experiences and our beliefs." For those witches who have a dilemma about cursing, she gave the following advice: "Look within yourself to see if it is part of your religion to accept cursing, hexing, jinxing, and crossing." She then clarified that she believed that these things do not make someone a bad or evil person. Though she speaks so confidently to her nearly two hundred thousand followers on YouTube, her listeners need to ask why anyone should think she is an authority on the matter.

---

[4] This is an encouraging admission, and one which Christians must be aware of when they seek to evangelize witches and help lead them into the Church.

[5] An expletive was used here; she meant "don't put up with nonsense from people."

Nonetheless, her followers, as the likes and comments indicate, are heeding her advice as if she is.

Lola addressed various aspects of cursing such as the issue of those who desire to manifest negative energy (i.e., a curse) and send it directly to someone, instead of only sending it *back* at the sender of a curse, which she says is preferred. In doing so, she touched on the issue of wounds, a key element that drives many people into the occult to begin with, as discussed in *The Rise of the Occult*. She stated, "This [desire to curse] usually comes from a place of hurt, where you have been wronged. It does not make you a bad person, it means you want justice for something that's happened. As far as I am concerned, that is completely fine." Lola also stated, "Though 'negative' [workings] seems to have a bit more kickback than 'positive,' 'you do you'," she said, adding, "There is no morality stopping you from seeking negative effects on other people." "Most of the time," she added, "[a curse] is done as retaliation: spells designed to send negative energy *back* to someone, returning it *back* to the original person who harmed them. Thus, it is not 'black magic'." She explained her logic further, stating, "In my case, most of this type of working that I do is to bind their negativity, is to send it back to them, and sometimes to send it back to them *amplified*. Now," she asked, "does that make me an evil person? That's really up to you, but as far as I'm concerned, it does not make me a bad person for me to want to send their toxic negativity right back at them again."

Those Who Embrace Cursing

There are certain occultic groups that embrace cursing without hesitation. In their 1989 interview with Bob Larson, Satanists Zeena and Nikolas Schreck[6] explained, "We believe in vengeance. We don't believe in turning the other cheek. If you are wronged in some way, you take it out with the person responsible – directly or indirectly." *Directly* would be a personal confrontation with the person while

---

[6] As a reminder, though they are by no means Christian, each has formally renounced Satanism since the time of that interview, but their views quoted here represent the beliefs of the Church of Satan at that time. However, these views survive to the present day, as depicted in the interview of Ciaran Lyons with Satanist David Sinclair Smith, conducted in February 2021.

indirectly would be through a "destruction ritual." Zeena added, "You seem to have this idea that we toss around these destruction rituals right and left, that we do them 'every Friday night' with no regard, pick a few [random] people out. Don't you think there's a reason why we have that?"[7]

Assuming Zeena was being honest about the restraint they exercise with these rituals, it does not mean that restraint is the norm. As Msgr. Rossetti pointed out, one of the exorcists on his team helped a young woman named "Sarah," whose mother was a Satanic priestess and introduced Sarah to witchcraft. He said, "Sarah said each week six witches gathered to curse priests and the bishops by name. They sat around an effigy of the priest and ritually cursed him. She added that there were many covens in her area, and all were weekly cursing different priests."[8]

To make a very important point in their conversation, Larson read again from the Satanic Bible: "Mad dogs are destroyed. The fact remains, given the opportunity, they would destroy you. Therefore, you have every right to symbolically destroy them, and if your curse provokes their actual annihilation, rejoice that you have been instrumental in ridding the world of a pest. He is made to be trampled underfoot." In response to this reading, Zeena said, "Of course we mean that...What do you think we would use a destruction ritual for? It's to destroy, obviously." Zeena then added, "If your wife is raped and murdered and you don't know who did it and you want to throw a random curse at whoever it was that did it, and if it works, shouldn't you be happy?"[9]

The Dark Side

Underlying all occult rituals is a dangerous reality: there is *no good* in the occult. Occultists profess that neither good nor evil exist. In practice, what this means is that the fallen human will of the occult practitioner is the only arbiter of whether it is acceptable to curse or to "bless," to do this or to do that. Subjective interests always win out. In the end, this means the systems of occult practice

---

[7] Occult Demon Cassette. "The First Family of Satanism [VHS]." *YouTube*, 24 June 2014. youtube.com/watch?v=uRf-FyDfRY0: Larson video #1.

[8] St. Michael Center for Spiritual Renewal blog, June 26, 2022, Diary #196.

[9] Larson video #1.

always tend toward corruption. Those, for example, who might begin in the occult seeking to be "good witches" quickly learn that this concept is a complete farce.[10]

Philomena gave the example that, in Thelema and in the Church of Satan, rituals often involve acts of impurity and the use of blood. This is also evident in rituals of the currently popular organized Satanic group known as The Satanic Temple (TST).[11] Life, for them, is expendable, Philomena said. She added that there is no true organization of ritual in the occult. There is no playbook for the routine and ritual, and practitioners end up building their own system and mimicking each other. In the occult, Helena said, "There is a lack of community; there is distrust: everyone is out for themselves and will harm you without much thought, as there is no concept of 'sin'."

In the realm of Satanism, an example of the corrupted reasoning behind curses is seen in Bob Larson's 1989 interview with Zeena and Nikolas Schreck. They addressed the matter when discussing the issue of the morality of what are called "destruction rituals."[12] Larson asked, "What if you are mistaken, and your selfish ego blinded you to the fact that it was not the other person who was guilty but actually you." Nikolas answered, "What's wrong with the selfish ego – I would think your selfish ego is a healthier gauge of reality than some moral system founded on a two-thousand-year-old book." Nikolas said they have to follow their gut instincts, as animals. "We are beasts," he added, "and we have to decide from gut instinct whether we have been wronged or not." Larson asked, referring to a hypothetical situation where a moral conclusion is made, "What if you are wrong?" Nikolas responded, "What is 'right and wrong'? In our case, we are making up our reality – we decide what is right and wrong."[13]

Hatred, expressed with the intent to harm and other forms of malice, is critical to the supposed power of certain spells. Fr. Ermatinger, in his book *The Trouble with Magic*, said, "Handbooks

---

[10] This will be discussed further below.

[11] For example, the rituals of SatanCon 2022, including their Impurity Ball and Invocation of the New Creative Aeon.

[12] This is something that organized Satanists, even "psychological, metaphorical, atheistic" types, engage in.

[13] Larson video #1.

for witchcraft, grimoire, indicate the relative efficacy and gravity of the harm done to others [is] in proportion to the hatred with which the curse is made."[14] This warning parallels the admission of Wiccans, witches, and Satanists that good and evil, black magic and white magic, are all arbitrary and nonexistent distinctions. Among other things, this means that those who embrace the occult are likely to be animated by hatred but not admit to it or be fearful of its negative consequences. As one popular witchcraft site stated, "All magic is part of the same energy," adding that the divisions that have become popularized are not real. This website rejected the idea of "white and black magic" in the same way that it rejected "good and evil." Both, it said, are human concepts but not real divisions. The witch Lola said the same thing as well. One of the important realizations for the youth who are getting into witchcraft is that, given the lack of a real distinction between black and white magic, there is also no such thing as a "white witch," despite what they might think.

The Occult: It's All Satanic

In the interview with Zeena and Nikolas Schreck when they were still members of the Church of Satan, Bob Larson proposed this very interesting and important point: that there is no such thing as a "good witch" or a "white witch."

Larson, referencing Anton LaVey's condemnation of the claim by some occultists that they themselves are "good witches" or "white witches," simplified the matter with the statement, "A witch is a witch is a witch," to which Zeena replied, "That's right." Nikolas chimed in, stating, "In a sense, that the act of manipulating and using the will and using ritual to create change is, by any definition, '*Satanic,*' anyone who does that is at least an *ipso facto* Satanist. So, these witches that say they're *good* witches, *white* witches, *nice* witches, are as hypocritical as a Christian."[15] Larson, to clarify the point further, added, "To me, your father [Anton LaVey] also says, of the Satanic witch, [in reference to psychics who say, 'God gave me this gift'] 'these people are playing the devil's game but refusing to

---

[14] Ermatinger, *Trouble with Magic*, 61.
[15] Larson video #1.

use the devil's name'." Zeena answered, "Wouldn't you consider any form of divination or faith healing or tarot reading…" "Divination is biblically forbidden," Larson interrupted, adding, "I would consider it to be Satanic." Zeena, agreeing, added, "So, we would say that anything that would fall under that category would be considered *Satanic*."[16]

Exorcist Msgr. Rossetti agrees with this perspective. He said, "Asking a witch or shaman to grant you a favor, such as healing or wealth or having another fall in love with you, is tantamount to making a deal with Satan. Such a deal will never end well."[17] Adelaide commented on the fact that the terms *right-hand path* and *left-hand path* are often used in magic to refer to the *white* and the *dark* magic. The lie, she said, is that the right-hand path of white magic is good and safe, but the truth is that they are the two hands of the same mystical body of Satan, so to speak. "Witches," she said, "all say, 'I only practice white magic!' They all believe it; I did."

One way to see that this is true is to realize that the language of the New Age, Wicca, and witchcraft is the same language as that used by Satanism. There is a good example in a statement by Satanist David Sinclair Smith in his interview with Ciaran Lyons. When they were preparing for Ciaran to do a ritual with him, David said, "This is the time, in this formalized way, to channel and harness that goal and make it manifest."[18] *Channel* and *manifest* and *harness*: the language of all forms of the occult, referring to the energy that they seek to manipulate through the art of spells and magic and ritual and will.

To further illustrate this reality, consider the following example. A witchcraft and Wicca website discussed the fact that atheists can also be Wiccans. It stated, "Wiccans hold reverence for Nature and accept the existence of a Goddess and/or God," but it then added that atheists can also practice "spirituality without religion." The goal here is to "connect with your *inner world* and *awaken the powers* that live within you. You don't need to seek out any Higher Beings because you can always find your Witchcraft inwards through deep

16 Larson video #1.
17 Rossetti, *Diary*, 131.
18 7NEWS Spotlight. "'SATANISTS NEXT DOOR' | Our cameras capture a secret ritual as a 'curse' is cast | 7NEWS Documentary." *YouTube*, 27 February 2021. youtube.com/watch?v=Wqa5F6vWWXM: Ciaran Lyons video.

meditation."[19] The language here directly mirrors Nikolas Schreck's comment below that Satanic magic does not pretend to "appeal to a higher force," as well as the Satanic belief that we are gods unto ourselves. If an atheist can tap into the same power as a Wiccan without believing in any of the gods and spirits that Wiccans rely upon, that indicates that the true power, even for a typical Wiccan, is not in the power of gods and spirits but in *themselves* as gods. It is "your inner world" that contains the "powers" that you seek in order to practice your witchcraft. The apprentice of Satan is the one who mirrors his self-glorification, rejecting all religious authority that might otherwise be superior to him, and exalting himself in the place of God and of power itself.

Real Evil Behind the Show of Ritual

In 1989, Nikolas Schreck defined black magic as "the use of will and ritual combined to create change in the world, without any restraint on what that change might be, and no hypocritical pretending that we are appealing to a higher force." Though, as a member of the Church of Satan at the time, he would have admitted to the belief that all the rituals they embrace are merely for show, and the names and images merely metaphorical and archetypal, members of the Church of Satan today, though likely also even in Nikolas Schreck's time, while using the same language, do connect these ritual to the existence of real "dark forces."[20] When Satanist David took Ciaran deep into the woods in 2021 to perform a ritual for Ciaran's personal interests,[21] he explained to Ciaran that, despite the emphasis that it was mere psychodrama, the ritual would indeed *summon* something. He explained, "Here's where the fantasy comes into play. Amongst the candles and the flames and the ambience of the forest – trust me, you'll get this primitive, primal feeling of like, 'there's other things out here'." Shifting to the proper attire of black, he explained, "Also, part of the ritual, if you can, wear black, all black, because you're channeling the forces of darkness."[22]

---

[19] *Emphasis* mine.
[20] In 2011, Nikolas admitted that, during this period, he was in fact a "blood-drinking theistic devil worshipper." See page 86.
[21] For more from that story, see *The Rise of the Occult*, 175.
[22] Ciaran Lyons video.

After the ritual which Ciaran himself joined, David further explained his approach, saying, "Just focusing your subconscious, and making it manifest in your subconscious, so, it's just going to start appearing and things will start manifesting in the real world. You'll start thinking, 'Hang on, is that just coincidence?' Just go with it, don't question it. Indulge, man, that's what all is about." One of the problems with this wild indulgence in dabbling with unseen entities, as Dr. Richard Gallagher explained, is that these "forces," in the history of the world, have always been understood to be potentially dangerous. He said, "From the dawn of history, ancient cultures clearly believed that the spirit world, however defined, was often hardly benign."[23] As a result, and likely acknowledged by all occultists deep down, there is a potential danger to everything they are doing…and they're fine with that.[24] This willingness greatly increases the spiritual danger and damage they will encounter.

Exorcists confirm this danger. Related to curses, Fr. Fortea said, "A demon is never invoked in vain." What he meant by this was that the invocation of a demon (i.e., any deity or entity) through a spell or a curse will always cause harm, and this primarily to the occultist. He added, "Whoever *does* the curse will be the first one affected by the demonic."[25] Msgr. Rossetti added, "Priests (or anyone) living a solid Christian life of sacraments and virtue are largely protected from the curse of a witch, although some harassment is possible. We exorcists just assume we are being regularly cursed. If one steps out from under the Church's protection and/or strays into sin, the curses can more easily take root and cause havoc."[26] Occultists, issuing curses and often a victim of them, all the while exposed to the "weather" of this fallen world subjected to the influence of the fallen angels, will experience first-hand this havoc merited by the malicious casting of curses.

---

[23] Dr. Richard Gallagher, *Demonic Foes* (New York, Harper One, 2020), 166.

[24] As seen, for example, in the practice among witches of doing spells and rituals to protect themselves when summoning deities or calling upon energies. Christians, on the contrary, do not enter into a wild spiritual realm when they pray to the One True God. When they are in His presence in prayer, any spiritual enemy will flee, save for the extraordinary allowances of Divine Providence, by which God seeks only to bring about more abundant spiritual goods and holiness.

[25] Fr. Jose Antonio Fortea, *Interview with an Exorcist* (West Chester: Ascension Press, 2006), 111.

[26] St. Michael Center for Spiritual Renewal blog, June 26, 2022, Diary #196.

Chapter Eight

Abortion is an Occult Ritual

This Chapter addresses a very dark aspect of occult practice. While the issue is such, the following presentation does not include specific details. Sensitive readers may still find some of the material difficult to reflect on, though the average reader should not have an issue.

A prominent element of evil within the occult involves sexual deviancy and general licentiousness, manifesting in many forms, varying in danger and destructiveness. Rituals, spells, and occult gatherings are often characterized by the presence of these types of perversity. As will be discussed, this spills over into the ritualistic use of abortion by the occult.

Sexual perversity is not limited to the darker realms of the occult, but is also an aspect of more mainstream practices, such as Yoga and the New Age. Alex Frank, from his experience in the Yoga world, said he saw a lot of people who got into modern "neo-tantra," which included sex parties, as well as drugs. "The visible appearance of Yoga is very alluring," he said. Though he went deep into it for health and spiritual reasons, he initially saw it as a great place to meet women. Gabriel, from his experience in the New Age, stated that, during the same time that he was at the high point in this occult study and practice, he was also dealing with an addiction to pornography.

The Satanic Black Mass, a key ritual within all forms of Satanism, is a hyper-sexualized ritual that entails a high degree of perversion. As Satanists in 1989, Zeena and Nikolas Schreck both stated clearly that they have no problem with nude people on occult altars for rituals. They did not discuss the Black Mass specifically, but one can deduce this was one of the rituals to which they were referring. Even so-called *atheistic* Satanism embraces sexual perversion and is not shy about it. In a Newsweek article[1] from

---

[1] *Newsweek*, October 29, 2021, "Orgies, Harassment, Fraud: Satanic Temple Rocked by Accusations, Lawsuit."

October of 2021, titled "Orgies, Harassment, Fraud: Satanic Temple Rocked by Accusations, Lawsuit," very revealing accusations of hedonism are presented against The Satanic Temple (TST), an organization that tries to market itself as rational and atheistic, steering clear of the "problems" of organized religions and of *actually* being Satanic. David Alan Johnson, the former social media editor for the TST chapter impacted by the internal lawsuit, was one of four members being sued by TST. As the article stated, "While digging up facts for their defense, they've run into other aggrieved Satanists around the country who have a litany of complaints about the organization, including allegations of sexually deviant gatherings that, according to one TST memo, allow for 'orgies, BDSM, ... ritual flogging, live ritual sex, burlesque show'." In July of 2020, the TST chapter Facebook page suggested ways to celebrate Lupercalia, which included, "Rituals with mock sacrifice, orgies, BDSM," and others. TST does not deny the accusation of approving "official orgies," but only denies that they are compulsory. Instead, TST issued "sex positive guidelines" to make sure no one felt uncomfortable or coerced to participate if these activities occurred at a TST event. Two years later, at *SatanCon 2022*, hosted by TST in Scottsdale, AZ, the celebration of sexual perversion was on display in the form of the "Impurity Ball" and another evening ritual.

Sexual Perversion, SRA, and Abortion

Sexual perversity in the context of the occult leads to what is known as Satanic Ritual Abuse (SRA). Sexual perversity and SRA both, of course, can lead to pregnancy. Pregnancy in the life of many modern members of our post-Christian pre-Satanic society, and within the occult itself, very often leads to abortion.

Geraldo Rivera, in his 1988 documentary on Satanism, he interviewed a group of nine well-known therapists from across the country who openly discussed threats they had personally received or had heard about happening against therapists who took claims of SRA seriously. One doctor said, "I have direct knowledge of both death threats on a therapist and an attempt to end the therapist's life, which was unsuccessful." One of the therapists interviewed, Dr. George Greaves, said, "Therapists have been directly threatened in ways that are quite alarming to them." Dr. Richard Kluft said, "The patient indicated to me that she wished to sacrifice the child with which she was pregnant. Naturally, I wasn't too enthusiastic about this. Shortly after this occurred, I started to get telephone death threats." Dr. Corydon Hammond said, "One of the things that I would add is that we are now hearing these reports from literally hundreds of therapists in every part of the United States." Dr. Greaves added, "Someone out there is telling us to back off."[2]

As Dr. Gallagher revealed from his own interviews with a Satanic "princess," SRA is a real thing, and it is intended to be just the first part of a greater ritual. As he wrote in his book, quoting this Satanist, "I was the cult's main breeder," she said. "I could get pregnant easily, which gave me a special status in the group. We had someone who could perform abortions, a physician's assistant, I think, a repulsive guy. We used fetuses for ceremonies. Daniel [the leader] encouraged it and said he and Satan would honor and reward me greatly for the 'service' and be eternally grateful for my role."[3] Rivera, in his documentary, also interviewed many women who testified that they were breeders for Satanic cults and their children were dedicated to Satan at birth and sacrificed in rituals. When he asked the obvious and rhetorical question, "And you *did* that?" one woman responded, "I was told it was the highest honor I could ever do as a woman, to sacrifice my [child]. I was so brainwashed; I believed their philosophy."[4] Adam Blai discussed the same reality. He said that one of the three types of people that those in exorcism ministry generally see is "mothers who are having off-the-books pregnancies for the [occultic] group and flee to protect their baby before it is born."[5] Likewise, Lucy admitted to me, "It took me a while to realize that abortion was demonic. I had one when I was younger, and it was a slow process in me realizing that it was a bad thing. Now I'm aware that it is about child sacrifice and most definitely demonic."

Thankfully, in some countries, abortion advocacy is not even allowed for discussion. Fr. Louis said that, in his home country in

---

[2] Available on YouTube. "The Geraldo Rivera Show: Devil Worship – Exposing Satan's Underground." October 22, 1988.
[3] Gallagher, *Demonic Foes*, 57.
[4] Geraldo documentary.
[5] Blai, Adam. *Hauntings, Possessions, and Exorcisms* (Emmaus Road Publishing, Steubenville, 2017), 25.

Africa, it is taboo to promote or support abortion publicly. "If you were to tell your parents you are going to have an abortion, or you were to stand up and celebrate abortion, the culture and the people would look at you as if you are mad!" Even politicians cannot push for it, he added. It cannot be a topic and is not tolerated at all.

Modern man often forgets that child sacrifice to demons is neither new nor unheard of in the history of humanity. In the Old Testament, particularly with the demon Moloch,[6] but also others, we read of many accounts of the barbaric practice of sacrificing babies to demons. Even the Israelites themselves, when they wandered from the One True God, resorted to this practice, enticed as they were by their pagan neighbors. Today, when the world at large has begun wandering from the One True God, we should not be surprised that the practice of child sacrifice should return.[7]

Idolatry and sexual deviancy are grave spiritual crimes, as the Church teaches and as exorcists note from their work. Fr. Athanasius pointed out that sins against the First and Sixth Commandments[8] are why people need exorcisms the most. These two Commandments are very connected and sins against either will compromise the entire person. Sins against both of these Commandments are recorded in the story of the second Fall, when Israel rejected God in the wilderness and worshipped the golden calf. Reading this account, it is clear, as Fr. Athanasius stated, that this is a situation of both idolatry and sexual deviancy in the form of a cultic orgy. It is important to note that both of these sins are characteristic of occult practices.

Interestingly, regarding the above topics, TST has taken two notable approaches. Through an operation known as "Grey Faction," it seeks to discredit most reports of SRA and, not surprisingly, has issued statements seeking to discredit each of the therapists mentioned above who were featured in Rivera's documentary, in addition to others who have been involved in some public way with this issue. TST has also become very publicly in favor of abortion,

---

6 Or "Molech" in the RSVCE translation.
7 Recall the modern push, in California, to encourage children to pray to ancient Aztec gods, who also demanded human sacrifice. See *The Rise of the Occult*, page 38.
8 "I am the Lord your God; you shall not have other strange gods before Me" and "You shall not commit adultery."

referring to it as a "religious abortion ritual" and arguing that it is a protected practice under "religious freedom."

Abortion is an Occultic Ritual

Abortion, which is widespread and vigorously protected by many in power today, is diabolical and, as exorcists affirm, calls down divine punishment on the country that protects abortion with its laws. Kyle Clement, who works with the exorcist Fr. Chad Ripperger at *Liber Christo*, did a great interview with Jesse Romero where he discussed the evil of abortion.[9] Abortion, which many outspoken Christians and former occultists have already identified as a Satanic sacrifice, is a huge element in the occult-infected regions of Hollywood and the government. This is not a "conspiracy theory" statement but, yes, it is so shocking that some people might not want to believe it is true, not because there is no evidence to support the claim but mainly because they do not *want* it to be true. The video above discusses the presence of Satanic rituals and ritualistic immorality, and the means by which many in Hollywood are exposed to it and compelled to take part in it in order to find success. Instead of delving into all the details here, as disturbing and enlightening as they are, I will leave it to those readers who would like to know more about this to view the video themselves.

Abortion, Kyle said, is a jealously guarded and vehemently defended powerful occult practice. It acquires great power and influence for those who offer this *blood sacrifice* and for those who ensure, by supporting it in law, that it is offered throughout the country. This power involves a greater ability to have their requests granted by the diabolical. Remember that Satan is described in Sacred Scripture as the "Prince of this World," possessing control over kingdoms and capable of giving power over them to those whom he chooses. One of his great demons in Sacred Scripture, Moloch, demanded the sacrifice of children. Our nation, according to exorcists, through the acceptance and celebration of abortion, has essentially submitted itself to this demon.

---

[9] Jesus 911. "The Most Evil Woman in the World," *YouTube*, May 7, 2020, youtube.com/watch?v=krLGDzFdbR4. Disturbing but very enlightening.

Example One: Abortion as a Satanic Ritual

In response to the beginnings of more restrictive legislations against abortion in the United States, TST came up with an "abortion ritual," clearly stating that this ritualized abortion is a Satanic ritual of their religion. TST's flyer about this abortion ritual includes a "personal affirmation" which sounds diabolically similar to the words of Consecration from the Mass. It says, "By my body, my blood my will, it is done." This element fits in with the tendency of the occult to invert the good and the holy. The TST abortion ritual flyer says that the ritual, which is not elaborate outside of the actual killing of the unborn child, says that "what is essential is the spirit and general intent." The Satanist is instructed to, first, look at her reflection, remember she is responsible to herself alone, and "focus on your intent," which is never clearly explained. Since it is a Satanic ritual, like a witchcraft spell, it is offered for and with some specific *intention*, but that is never clear in the ritual, though it seems the intent is to "affirm your autonomy and free will." She is then instructed to recite the third and fifth tenets of TST, which state "one's body is inviolable, subject to one's will alone" and, paraphrasing, "one should follow clear scientific facts in forming beliefs." The first is clearly Satanic[10] and the second is clearly hypocritical.[11] The abortion, whether surgical or chemical, is then performed. Since the actual abortion is a key part of the ritual, the Satanist concludes the ritual afterward, looking at her reflection again and reciting her "personal affirmation" again.

Example Two: Ritualized Abortion

A woman, steeped in either the New Age or witchcraft, created a course to guide women in performing a "self-guided abortion in a sacred manner."[12] In the course, comprised of video presentations,

---

[10] Due to the exaltation of the will over God and Truth.

[11] Due to the abundance of scientific facts pertaining to the personhood and separate humanity of the unborn child in the womb.

[12] From a website called Selfguidedabortion. The video was called "What is a Sacred, Empowered Abortion". The video, and the YouTube account with it, were later taken down for "violating YouTube's Community Guidelines." Public testimonies about utilizing abortion in witchcraft rituals are becoming more common. Many witches also admit that there is a human life being sacrificed as part of the ritual.

she clearly presented abortion as a sacred ritual and even guided the viewer in how to create an altar for the abortion. She never referred to the child directly, though appeared to acknowledge the child's humanity, and often referred to the abortion as a "sacred experience." Interestingly, YouTube took down the account that posted this video for violating some of its "guidelines." Providentially, I was able to view the video and take notes on it before this removal occurred.

The woman incorporated sage and other kinds of incense to "cleanse the energy and bless" both the altar for the abortion and the abortion pills themselves, which she also placed on the altar. This "blessing" was to allow the one who conducted this ritual to "put your intention for healing into the pills before you take them." She lit a candle and placed a tarot card on the altar, which symbolized feminine fertility and feminine energy. Speaking to any woman who was conducting this ritual, she instructed the woman to have a sacred container in which they will place the "products of conception or the fetal remains," and save it for later, "when we find a way to bury or otherwise properly dispose of the fetal remains in a way that gives reverence and respect and support to this sacred abortion experience." Take note of the use of the word "bury," and that this burial *gives reverence* not to the *child* but to the *sacred abortion experience.*

The woman then stated that the ritual for the abortion not only helps with the emotions that arise from the abortion but also "opens up new potentials and possibilities into our lives." This disturbing aspect of the "sacred abortion" is further explained. The logic of the sacredness of abortion is, she said, "The awareness that energy cannot be destroyed; energy can only be transformed into something new and, in that sense, the container of your sacred abortion invites you to understand that the *energy of your pregnancy* can only be *transmuted* into something new, and it invites you to decide: what do you want to *manifest* into your own life and create in the wake of this abortion experience? What newness can still be birthed from you through the experience of this abortion?"

Her use of the term "transmuted" is very revealing. According to Merriam-Webster, "transmute" means, "to change or alter in form, appearance, or nature and especially to a higher form." Her explanation of this ritual abortion is clearly revealing that it can be used to the *advantage* of the woman. Abortion is seen, by this woman, as an occultic ritual by which she may obtain a powerful *energy* with which to *manifest* something new, thus bettering herself and her own life. She further explained that a "sacred abortion" allows women to "make peace in our hearts" and enables them to "move forward in our lives in an integrated fashion." Here she highlighted the *danger* of the abortion, which has the power to "fracture ourselves and our whole selves through trauma." Making the abortion a "*sacred* abortion" avoids this fracturing and transforms the abortion into a ritual "that makes us more rich and interesting and full as an individual."

She added that ritualizing the abortion takes the abortion, and the injury that she admitted it brings (by her repeated use of the word "healing") and creates healing for that injury and gives meaning to the abortion. The healing from the injury of abortion, though she never uses the word "injury," can take "days, weeks, or even years." The whole time she spoke of "healing," she never mentioned "healing from" or "wound" or "injury" except the one use of the word "trauma," as mentioned above. At the same time, she always spoke of "healing" in a notably subdued, calm, and tranquilized voice, deceptively masking that the abortion is a violent procedure to the child and to the mother's body and mind, even if done with pills alone.

Example Three: Blessing Abortion

A baby-killing center, *Whole Women's Health of South Bend*,[13] boasted, on May 12, 2022, "This abortion clinic is now blessed," after they invited a group of "local religious leaders to bless our Indiana clinic and honor the sacred work of our clinic staff." Apparently, this is "part of a long tradition of progressive faith communities." These communities included United Church, Catholics for Choice, United Methodist, ELCA, and Unitarian.[14] From the video of the event, one of the "faith leaders" said, "I thank God for giving me the strength to be here today and I thank God for this place that is allowing women to come to a safe place."

---

[13] *Whole Women's Health Alliance*, September 2017, "This Abortion Clinic is Now Blessed."
[14] Twitter post on May 16th, 2022, under the name "GaryMillrat."

In Austin, TX, in 2019,[15] a similar incident was reported by HuffPost in an article titled, "Interfaith clergy gather to bless Texas abortion clinic and its staff." These religious leaders included Christians, Jews, and others. It was organized by Religious Coalition for Reproductive Choice (RCRC), Texas Freedom Network, and Whole Women's Health. The founder of Labyrinth Progressive Student Ministry walked through the building like a normal patient would, "praying for peace in each room," and burning sage. In a picture in the article, an old woman stands in a nondescript striped blouse, pointing a sage bundle at a frame on the wall, standing in a room with a patient bed and medical computer table. Speaking to Religion News Service, "Rev." Katey Zeh, executive director of RCRC, said they believe abortion is "sacred work," adding, "The Whole Woman's Health clinic in Austin is also a blessed space, not only because of our ritual of blessing on Tuesday but because providing reproductive health services has always been sacred work." "Rev." Amelia Fulbright, a campus minister in Austin, told Huffington Post, "As people of faith, it's not that we think we're bringing God to this place; we believe God is already present in that space...But it's to ask for prayers of safety, healing and peace, to infuse the space with an *energy* that is life-giving for women, a lot of whom are in an anxious time."[16] This sort of ceremony is also reported to have occurred in San Antonio, TX in October of 2019. Texas Freedom Network stated, "Clinic blessings are a relatively new but growing phenomenon." As with the other incident, "Catholics for Choice" participated in the occult ritual.[17]

In 2018, according to the Washington Post,[18] clergy gathered to bless "one of the only [*sic*] U.S. abortion clinics performing late-term abortions." Part of the prayer led by "Rev." Carlton Veazey included the words, "Keep [the doctors, nurses, and patients] safe and keep them strong. And may they always know that all that they

---

[15] *HuffPost*, July 10, 2019, "Interfaith Clergy Gather To Bless Texas Abortion Clinic And Its Staff."

[16] *LifeNews*, July 11, 2019, "Christian and Jewish Clergy Bless Abortion Clinic: Claim God is Present in This Space." *Emphasis* mine.

[17] *Texas Freedom Network*, October 2, 2019, "Joint Press Release: Faith Leaders in McAllen: 'Bless this Clinic'."

[18] *Washington Post*, January 29, 2018, "Clergy Gather to Bless An Abortion Clinic Which Provides Rare Late Term Abortions in Bethesda."

do is *for Thy glory.*"[19] Four Christian pastors, one rabbi, and a Hindu priest were invited to the ritual. Veazey also added that "God affirms a woman's moral agency" to choose abortion. Some form of ritual water was sprinkled in every room of the clinic as well as the parking lot. There were representatives from the RCRC in attendance, so it was likely the same ritual that they perform.

The Religious Coalition for Reproductive Choice[20]

According to a *Vice* article in May of 2018,[21] the RCRC is comprised of different religious beliefs, ranging from "Catholicism, Islam, and Hinduism to Earth-centered spirituality." It stated that "RCRC-affiliated clergy in religious garb can be seen serving as clinic escorts." Dr. Jackson, of the executive management team for RCRC, said that not only is "a woman's right to choose…sacrosanct," but "the place of decision-making that women enter before they walk across the threshold of a clinic is sacred." At the RCRC's own website, under "Clinic Blessings," the viewer is greeted by a prominent image of a woman wearing a flowing red garment, gesturing upward dramatically, as if summoning, or beckoning, a spiritual energy. The blessing ritual includes a "diverse reading from sacred texts," rituals, the burning of sage, "cleansing water," some bland elements, and other things not publicly revealed. In a document on their website, "Prayers and Meditations," a "Protestant Prayer" sacrilegiously quotes St. Paul, saying, among other things, "Therefore, I cling to the promise that there is nothing that can separate me from your love in Christ Jesus."

FaithChoiceOhio posted a story in 2018 titled, "Religious Group Blesses Columbus Abortion Clinic to Show Support for Care."[22] In that article, it stated that, though this was the first clinic blessing in Columbus, there had already been one in Cleveland, and the group planned six more for 2019. Included in the ritual was the testimony of a young woman who chose to abort two children before the age of twenty. Stating that she felt God's presence with her when she had

[19] Thus, they pray to a god who loves the slaughter of babies. *Emphasis* mine.
[20] RCRC.org > Clinic Blessings.
[21] *Vice.com*, May 20, 2018, "The Religious Coalition Blessing Abortion Clinics Across America."
[22] November 10, 2018.

the abortions, she added, "I have been blessed by God in so many ways. I have grown to be bold and unapologetic about my abortions." One "minister," praying to her deity to ask it to bless the clinic, stated, "You have empowered us to make decisions."

Chapter Nine

The Modern Satanic Movement

While it is not a comfortable thing for most people to think about, the times call for many Christians to acquire a basic understanding of the modern Satanic movement. People often react to the growing public presence of Satanic groups either with fear or with disbelief. Many see them as simply attention-seekers and regard them more as a political force than as a real religious movement. Christians react with fear or outrage or choose to pay no attention to them hoping they are just a small fringe movement that will have no impact on anyone. Unfortunately, it is not uncommon for an evil to arise in a generation which is too great for that generation to comprehend. Overwhelmed, and presently at a distance from that evil, they try to look the other way and hope it simply vanishes.

An analysis of the reality of modern Satanism is critical for many reasons. Much of modern public Satanism, though not all, presents itself as an atheistic enterprise that invokes only the *image* of Satan, not the demonic person, seeing in it a representation and a symbol of rebellion and liberty and autonomy. In this, they claim that they do not worship Satan and that they do not believe that any preternatural or supernatural realities actually exist. Their religious rituals are, they claim, merely psychological or cathartic or symbolic expressions of their goals and desires and personal beliefs. However, many in the Satanic community are witches as well. Many others grow tired of the psychodrama and "want the real thing," that is, to tap into real preternatural powers. Thus, the public image that Satanists are "atheistic" and "do not believe in the supernatural or preternatural" proves to be either a lie or to be true in their official structure but so unsatisfying of a concept that most of their members ignore it and begin invoking Satan and/or other entities, energies, or powers anyway. This is seen in the powerful example of Zeena Schreck, the daughter of Anton LaVey, who was once the Church of

Satan's most prominent spokesman and promoted LaVey's version of psychological and atheistic Satanism in the late 1980s. However, she eventually broke from this form of Satanism and sought "the real thing" in the Temple of Set, embracing a form of Satanism which venerated a real dark spiritual entity.[1]

Regarding the oft-repeated claim that "Satanists don't believe in the devil," there are a few ways to look at it that will help us see both the truth and the lie which this statement presents. First, this statement is only affirmed by certain forms of *atheistic* Satanism. Thus, many forms of Satanism actually *do* believe in the devil.[2] Second, the reality is that these atheistic Satanists, while rejecting a belief *in* the devil, actually come to *embody* the devil. They *become* the devil, in a sense. They act out the devil's role. They *are* the devil, in that sense. As a result, then, it could be said that they are members of Satan's "mystical body."[3] They replace the devil: they ignore his existence but assume his spirit at the same time. His spirit animates them but hides as it does; so, they take up his mind and his mindset, all the while denying he exists. In doing so, Satan replaces *them* and extends his reign and anger through them. They then speak with the same voice as their dark master, who likewise seeks to convince the world he does not exist.

Jesse Romero, author and speaker on spiritual warfare topics, made several relevant observations as a guest on the Taylor Marshall podcast, speaking about a large Catholic protest against *SatanCon* in February of 2022 in Scottsdale, Arizona, in which he had participated. From his interactions with them outside the convention, he said the Satanists he encountered repeated the claim that they don't worship Satan but simply see him as an anti-authority role model and as the rebel against oppression. However, Jesse pointed out that this is like a Christian saying, "I am a Christian, but I don't believe in Christ." He continued, explaining, "If Satanists don't believe in Satan, then why call themselves Satanists

---

[1] Even as a child, she was exposed to real witches and Satanists due to her affiliation with the Church of Satan.

[2] See Riaan Swiegelaar's comments on statistics of applications on p. 80.

[3] Fulton Sheen spoke about the "mystical body of Antichrist" in his book *Communism and the Conscience of the West*, 10. This present application is loosely based on that.

and invoke him?" Just like their "father,"[4] Romero added, they cannot be believed, for their nature is to deceive. Further, with their rejection of the Ten Commandments, and of any moral authority outside of themselves, what would stop them from lying about their intentions and beliefs? The values they celebrate proclaim, themselves, that they "do [their] father's desires"; they claim to promote freedom and autonomy, especially "bodily autonomy" (i.e., abortion), and Satan would very much do the same thing.

What is Satanism?

As the reader will see below, Satanism is not an honest religion, and not just in relation to what they really believe. While public leaders of the Satanic movement in the 1980s made efforts to separate themselves from the murderous Satanists in the news at the time, some also made, at that same time, statements indicating that they saw a real need to purge the planet of the "idiots" and the "unworthy."[5] These statements obviously embolden the *independent* Satanists who, likely mentally unstable and potentially already possessed, are inclined to do harm. Satan gladly accepts both the chaos *within* Satanism and the crazies it attracts. Ultimately, he is driving everyone mad who calls upon him and will use everything they give him in his destructive mission.

Part of the public presentation of their beliefs is the desire to make themselves appear to be "respectable" members of society. Anton LaVey, as depicted in Geraldo's 1988 documentary, said, "Most of the people that are in my group are professional people, they are businesspeople, they are people that are from very responsible walks of life."[6] Michael Aquino, the founder of the Temple of Set, in that same interview, said that the Satanism of the Temple of Set, is "ethical, above ground, positive." He added, in reference to the Satanic murderers that were brought forward in Geraldo's documentary, "All of these people come from a background

---

[4] "Why do you not understand what I say? It is because you cannot bear to hear my word. You are of your father the devil, and your will is to do your father's desires. He was a murderer from the beginning, and has nothing to do with the truth, because there is no truth in him. When he lies, he speaks according to his own nature, for he is a liar and the father of lies." (John 8:43-44)
[5] Bob Larson video #1, as quoted in full below.
[6] Geraldo documentary.

in which their moral and religious instruction has been from a religious tradition other than ours. In the Church of Satan and the Temple of Set, we have not had any problems with criminal behavior."[7] While, from my research, the Church of Satan and the Temple of Set are not taking a very public role today, The Satanic Temple is, and it is seeking to cast the same warm light on Satanism as did its diabolical forebears. As a result, we have a continuity, though not coordinated, in the effort exerted to present a rational and respectable face and persona to public Satanism, going back to the 1960s.

Satanism, like many forms of the occult, cannot be easily pinned down. For example, there is more than sufficient evidence to demonstrate that, even within a particular form of Satanism, there is very little uniformity in the beliefs and practices of their members. Given the fact that these groups are inspired by Satan, we should not expect anything different.[8] Also, the supposedly benign public versions of Satanism do not *officially* represent Satanism and have no control over Satanism. The unaffiliated versions, and those that spin off from these public groups, show the danger within any movement that invokes the devil.[9] For example, Elizabeth, who was once involved with a Satanist named Damien, said Damien was an "unaffiliated Satanist." "He made up his own stuff because," she said, "he thought everyone else was ridiculously wrong." Damien was violent, abusive, and likely perfectly possessed. He was narcissistic, sought to inspire terror in everyone, and was clearly dangerous. *Unaffiliated* Satanism, as Michael Aquino implied, might be the source of Satanic murders, but there is no way to disassociate those "renegades" from the "official" Satanic organizations when it comes to being inspired by a Satanic vision and philosophy. They are all part of the same philosophical and religious system, despite the appearance of divisions. We cannot separate the public "image-conscious" Satanism of the Church of Satan and TST from the unaffiliated Satanism since anyone who invokes the name of Satan

---

[7] Geraldo documentary.
[8] The Rite of Exorcism condemns Satan with various labels, such as "the foe of the human race, the traitor of nations, the source of discord, and the seducer of men."
[9] Plus, as Swiegelaar revealed, even within atheistic Satanism there are sixteen percent who are theistic Satanists. See below p.99.

shares in the guilt of those who embrace Satan and act in his name to carry out his will against God and man.[10]

Geraldo also interviewed convicted murderer and former Satanist Sean Sellers, a young man who murdered several people, and heard Sellers' thoughts on the "ethical" nature of the Church of Satan. He said, in response to Geraldo's question about Satanism's connection to his violent murders, "I've heard Dr. Aquino say that the [evil] ideals that we are talking about here are not Satanism. That's because Satanists believe that good is evil and evil is good and so, of course, they're not the ideals that he believes in. He believes that evil *is* good. That is what I believed in."[11]

The Satanic Bible

One of the means by which modern Satanism has influenced its followers is the book, *The Satanic Bible*, published in 1969. Geraldo and Larson were both able to get prominent Satanists to speak on the importance, and the interpretation, of this book. In Geraldo's documentary, Dr. Aquino had said the Satanic Bible was polemical and was not to be taken literally. In response to this, Sean Sellers said, "I am working with a sixteen-year-old boy now – and with ministries around the United States. He takes the Satanic Bible literally. I took it literally. A lot of people are taking the Satanic Bible literally." Just a year after Geraldo's documentary, in the interview conducted by Bob Larson, both Zeena and Nikolas Schreck quickly stated that the book speaks for itself. Zeena said, "It should be pretty self-explanatory. There's no hidden meaning." Nikolas added, "Unlike the Christian Bible, the Satanic Bible speaks for itself. It requires no scholars."[12] There is a critical contradiction, here, in the words of the spokesmen of these two otherwise very similar Satanic organizations.

Nikolas, who defended the Satanic Bible in the above statements from 1988, shared his revised perspective about the Satanic Bible in 2022, a perspective that removes all mysticism about this Satanic document. This book had become the basis of the first public Satanic organization, the Church of Satan, and the inspiration for many to

---

[10] See quote below by Nikolas on the danger of invoking Satan.
[11] Geraldo documentary.
[12] Larson video #1.

join it or take up for themselves this rising Satanic movement, both then and now. In 2022, Nikolas explained that, in the time of the occult fad following the release of the movie *Rosemary's Baby* in 1968, Avon Books, today an imprint of HarperCollins Publishers, heard about Anton LaVey and his founding of the Church of Satan and asked him to write a book.[13] That book became *The Satanic Bible*, which HarperCollins still publishes today. Nikolas spoke bluntly and dismissively about the book, saying it was simply "a pre-packaged deal; [the publishers said] just stick something in here and this is what the book will look like." Nikolas said he tried to work with LaVey on writing the book but found that LaVey lacked any discipline for writing. Since they had a contract with Avon Books, Nikolas said that Dianne, a member of the Church of Satan at the time, took their newsletters, called *The Cloven Hoof,* and some other things and put them together into one document. "They put in a lot of filler," Nikolas added. "If you look at it, there are a lot of placeholders in the book. It was a quickly-put-together paperback exploitation thing to cash in on *Rosemary's Baby*."[14] Despite the absence of any mystical significance to this book, it still has the power, in the evil of its words and its calls to action, to motivate men to rebel against God and His divine and natural laws.

Atheistic Satanism Embraces Ritual Satanism

John pointed out that the Church of Satan was the first group to be openly Satanic. On the surface, they claimed to be *atheistic,* that all of their rituals were purely *psychological,* and that Satan is only a *metaphor.* As John said, "That is the public face, what they sell to the public. This is 'entry level' 'baby' Satanism, but within that there are factions that practice all sorts of stuff."[15] There are multiple spin-offs from the Church of Satan, which are much less metaphorical and much more ritualistic, such as the Temple of the Vampire and the Temple of Set. The Temple of Set, for example, is more honest, John

---

[13] The interest among publishers was actually more complicated than this.
[14] The Nikolas Schreck Channel. "Nikolas Schreck Interviewed by Legs McNeil THE DARK SIDE OF THE SIXTIES PT 2 HOLLYWOOD SATANISTS," *YouTube,* April 17, 2022, youtube.com/watch?v=aIAqa-I0HjQ.
[15] This is further demonstrated by Riaan Swiegelaar's comments on the beliefs of Satanists within the group he co-founded.

said: they openly admit that they worship "the prince of darkness," but they give him the name "Set" instead. The "atheistic and metaphorical" Satanic group known as the Church of Satan, in the public testimony of David Sinclair-Smith, one of their members, has been shown to actually believe in *dark energy* and *forces* that impact and affect the world, despite their emphasis to the contrary. This indicates that they *do* believe in something that mirrors the activity of an invisible preternatural or supernatural reality. It would be important to also demonstrate, as far as possible, that the *current* public face of "atheistic" Satanism is functioning in the same way.

The current and most public face of "atheistic and metaphorical" Satanism is the group called The Satanic Temple. Throughout the world, there are approximately forty-one "congregations," thirty-eight of those being in the U.S. As of June 2022, there were over seven hundred thousand members.[16] John, as a former occultist after several decades of practice, holds the view that, while TST is a younger and more political group, claiming to be interested mainly in exposing the hypocrisy of Church and State issues, their atheistic emphasis is just a façade: they do worship Satan. "They're very careful," he added, "but the narcissism is going to reveal itself sooner or later. There are a lot of narcissists in these groups." While TST never admits to worshiping Satan, John's suspicions are likely due to the strong presence of witchcraft among TST's members. As John pointed out, some of the same witches that were publicly cursing Trump are members of TST,[17] which you can see from their social media accounts. They are also involved in BLM and other similar groups. He said the online cursing regarding Trump was very easy to see when he was in office. These witches and Satanists would jump into Twitter threads and issue curses right there, in the form of specific imagery and repeated lines from spells. This author once mentioned "Satanist" in a Tweet, discussing issues related to Satanists and to the decline of society, and the Twitter thread was inundated with these same disturbing images from Satanists and witches which, according to John, were related to curses.

---

[16] TheSatanicTemple.com/blogs/news/new-milestone-over-700-000-members. The Church of Satan does not, as a matter of policy, publicize the size of its membership.
[17] These curses were reported as early as 2017 and have endured at least up through 2021.

While declaring they do not worship Satan, TST admits to using black masses as one of their four main rituals,[18] though without providing a detailed description, other than what the name will convey to the reader. They also promote "unbaptisms," which will appeal to the rebellious occult-inclined youth who, often today, seek a way to remove or undo their baptism and, as a result, their Christian identity.[19] Like other Satanic groups and witches, TST also performs "destruction rituals." These, as they are presented publicly, are much more psychological than those of the Church of Satan and of witches. However, inspired as they are by Satan as the image of the *rebel*, a member of TST is free to deviate from TST rituals if he pleases, though that could lead to his removal from the group since the "tenets of TST" are supposed to govern these rituals. Further, as would be expected given the number of rituals they embrace, TST also ordains its own ministers. What this ordination ceremony entails is not public, but those who are ordained are given the authority to *create* official TST rituals. The list of rituals on their website does state that these are only "some" of the rituals they utilize.

The disconnect between the atheism TST claims to believe and the actual ritual practices and accompanying beliefs observed in reality can be noted within the book of Satanic ritual which TST promotes, called *The Devil's Tome: A Book of Modern Satanic Ritual*. Published in 2020 by the author, Shiva Honey, it contains a foreword from the founder of TST, Lucien Greaves, in which he repeats the public claim that TST is "non-theistic," is purely metaphorical in its use of ritual, and does not "advocate a belief in the supernatural," nor, it would seem, though they do not state it directly, any belief in preternatural beings or powers. However, Greaves also wrote that he has witnessed "ritual participants [of Satanism] enjoying profound religious experiences" which, to be clear, did not include "beliefs in supernatural powers." On the copyright page, it is stated that this book of rituals is not endorsed by TST, but Greaves refers to it in his foreword as "a record of what The Satanic Temple's rituals have been, as well as something of a ritual recipe book from

---

[18] Thesatanictemple.com/pages/faq.

[19] This, of course, is not possible. Baptism is the greatest gift from God which permanently changes the soul of the individual. This divine action cannot be undone by any human means.

which creative Satanists, ritually inclined, can derive inspiration for creating and conducting their own unique ritual events."[20]

The book also contains an introduction from the author. It is important to first understand her connection to TST. Shiva Honey is a Satanic Priestess and Ordained Minister of TST. She was a founding member of the first chapter of TST, in Detroit, and of The National Council of The Satanic Temple. She was the chief architect of the ritual for the unveiling of the Baphomet statue and the "Snaketivity" statue, as well as many other TST rituals. She was given a high award within TST for *The Devil's Tome.*

In the Introduction, she uses language that hints at Satanic rituals having much more than a metaphorical and psychological element. She said, "To me, Satanism is not about asserting power over others, but rather finding power within yourself." Ritual allows her, among other things, to "assert my will in everyday life." These rituals, she added, "Can give you tremendous power if you open yourself to it." The reader should recall the way in which Church of Satan member David Sinclair Smith spoke, and the way in which Andrew spoke as a Thelemite.[21] "Finding power within yourself" is aligned with Wicca; "assert my will" is aligned with Thelema; "give you tremendous power if you open yourself to it" is aligned with the Church of Satan rituals as depicted by David Sinclair Smith, which harness a dark energy and bring real manifestations of change in the world.

Further, Shiva Honey has a website in which she presents some of the rituals from her book and sells occult items to be used in these rituals. In the description of one of her rituals, she admits that some of the rituals, or the motivation within the rituals, come from a deep wound she carries. This is a critical admission.[22] In describing her ritual on self-love, she writes of the abuse she suffered from her father. She said she was taught to hate herself by her abusers and to see herself as ugly. "I still have the voices of my abusers echo in my head from time to time, and I still deal with body-image and self-esteem issues," she wrote on her website.[23]

---

[20] Honey, Shiva, *The Devil's Tome*, Serpentinae, March 25, 2020. Kindle edition.

[21] See *The Rise of the Occult.*

[22] See *The Rise of the Occult*, chapter Eight, on the connection between wounds and the occult.

[23] Serpentinae.com/writing/devotionsatanicritual.

In addition to this important admission, for which the reader should offer prayers, it is also clear that she sells many occult ritual items. The embrace of these ritual items seems to contradict TST's public statement that they do not believe in anything supernatural or preternatural. In addition to other things, she sells the following products, whose description should raise eyebrows in light of the claim that TST rituals are metaphorical and psychological only: "Temple fragrance and ritual oil" which is purported to "awaken...buried powers"; "Non Serviam ritual oil ... [which] was created to help you separate from toxic people and habits, ground yourself in your own protection and to build courage"; "The Witch Incense...[which] bestow[s] comfort and courage"; a "witch's spoon"; "The Witch's Cauldron... [which] is ideal for spell casting and burning rituals"; and "The Sight Sigil Patch" which is connected to her "sight ritual" in her book.

The language in the above examples is very similar to, if not exactly the same as, descriptions that can be found on a Wiccan or witchcraft website. As was discussed in *The Rise of the Occult*, some witches and Wiccans claim that a witch or Wiccan can be an atheist while still believing in the presence of a power or an energy which, whether flowing from the earth, the stars, the deities, or from within the witches themselves, can be utilized as a cause to bring about desired effects. Thus, it would seem that the *line* between psychological rituals and energy-manipulating rituals in atheistic Satanism is very thin, easily leading one away from mere psychological catharsis into real spirit summoning.

A current example and admission about the presence of true occultic Satanism inside otherwise "atheistic and metaphorical" Satanic groups comes from statements by Riaan Swiegelaar, a recent convert from Satanism and co-founder of his former organization, the South African Satanic Church (SASC). In a Facebook video from August 26, 2022, he spoke about how his organization started out as an archetypal form of Satanism, like the Church of Satan and TST, where Satan was just a metaphor of the eternal rebel. "How blinded I was and how deceived!" he said. "How much the devil is lying to [Satanists], thinking that the devil does not exist!" He said that the SASC tried to represent Satanism in a legitimate and above-board way in the beginning, similar to the statements of the founders of the other modern Satanic sects. After they launched their group,

Swiegelaar said lots of people started to join and lots of money came in through donations. Then, the SASC made the decision to allow any type of Satanist to join the group as members. Some of these individuals were admittedly *theistic* Satanists, "devil worshippers," as they called themselves, who knew clearly that Satan existed just as Christianity describes him, and they actually "worship him with everything they have," Swiegelaar said. When Swiegelaar left the SASC in 2022, there were about 12,100 members. He said that at least 2,000 of these were theistic Satanists. That means sixteen percent of the members of SASC were theistic Satanists who ritually worship the devil yet belong to a group that *publicly* proclaims they do not believe that Satan exists.[24]

Not Psychological After All

One thing that unites many sects of the occult is that the practitioner will very often begin with a belief that "none of this is real." This was the case for John in the beginning of his practice. It is also the case for many forms of modern Satanism. Further, and as many need to come to understand, it is also the case for Yoga. Many occult practitioners are ensnared by the initial belief that all of this occult ritual is psychological only, dealing with the mind and archetypes and similar purely mental and philosophical realities; nothing that has a true existence outside of your own mind. John's own story provided a perfect example of the eventual danger brought by embracing one of these "psychological" occultic practices. John first began to do rituals invoking the assistance of a demon when he summoned one that was supposed to teach him the archaic arts of astrology, something in which he was very interested. However, during the ritual, though he still believed it was all psychological, in the smoke rising from the incense on his altar he saw two eyes appear. It was then that he realized he was not simply tricking his own mind to believe something, but that there was a real presence with him in that room. When he knew it was all real, though, he jumped in completely: he made a pact with that demon

---

[24] Swiegelaar Facebook video, August 26, 2022. The videos he posted on Facebook have since been deleted.

and knew he had to keep going to the next level in order to attain more occult knowledge.

Zeena and Nikolas Schreck apparently progressed in the same way. When this topic came up in their second interview with Bob Larson,[25] they both agreed with Larson's description that they left the Church of Satan because it was "nothing more than atheistic psychodrama and the real thing was in the Temple of Set."[26] Current Church of Satan member, David Sinclair Smith, in his interview with Ciaran Lyons, repeated the wording of Zeena and Nikolas Schreck, stating, "Rituals first and foremost are what we call a psychodrama." However, he added, "When I call upon Satan, it just resonates and it channels a feeling. So, when I say, 'hail Satan!', it empowers, it makes me feel like I'm charging this energy, this dark force and nature in the universe, which is immense."[27] Despite emphasizing that it remains merely a "psychodrama," David attested to an "energy," a "dark force," which is "immense" and which "empowers" him. He also stated in the same interview with Ciaran that these rituals can bring about changes in the world, including apparently causing someone's death.[28]

Within the Satanism of the Church of Satan is the claim that there are no preternatural beings existent which can be called upon by the practitioner. However, this claim is an *illusion* because their own statements reveal that there is a *sort of* preternatural power that they actually do believe in, as was presented in the above example. The Church of Satan website itself admits to this. Within its beliefs is the idea that they are "I-theists," that they are the "God" of their own subjective universe. The rituals they conduct are "self-transformational psychodrama" to "purge oneself of unwanted emotional baggage" and as a means for "emotional stimulation." They admit, though, that "some Satanists also consider the possibility that" through these rituals and the "raising of emotions"

---

[25] Larson video #2.

[26] Nikolas Schreck had, in his first interview with Bob Larson, referred to Satan as an archetype. At this point he was a member of the Church of Satan. He later referred to the dark forces as his friends and peers.

[27] Ciaran Lyons video.

[28] As David told Ciaran when discussing his use of a destruction ritual. David stated that he used the ritual against some neighbors who were playing loud music. The two individuals who lived there hanged themselves shortly after his ritual. David's statements explaining the matter are quite chilling. See *The Rise of the Occult*, 176.

focused on a specific goal, "ideas/concepts/images might be transmitted to the minds of other people at a distance." They claim to believe that this may exist as a "part of nature," for which they find apparent support in the work of biologist Rupert Sheldrake.[29] This "part of nature" is very similar to other occultic groups who speak of an *energy* that is present in the universe and which can be manipulated.

These ideas lead the Church of Satan to admit that some Satanists "have found results [from their rituals] that they feel are beyond coincidence or statistical parameters." Further, they say that the Church of Satan does not seek to judge its members based on "their personal understanding of how ritual functions." In their advice to youth, the website states, "Don't be disturbed or frightened or think you're crazy when you feel at one with the Dark Ones you conjure forth, or by the magical results you begin to produce." Clarifying that this is still within the realm of "I-theist" behavior, it states, "You'll find that your 'daemonic guide' is an aspect within you – don't look for it outside. You just have to contact that part of yourself and listen to it."[30]

Shockingly to some, Yoga is very much like Satanism in this regard. Yoga professes to focus merely on archetypes as symbols of power, these being presented as "purely psychological" in their usage. Likewise, practitioners of Yoga use the same language as Satanists: psychological and archetypal which are also "energies" with real power to effect change. In the following example, attention should be paid to these similarities as well as to the progression from archetype to reality. *Yoga Journal,* in an article from October of 2008, titled "How to be Fierce," said that the "deities of yoga … serve as archetypes" and "personify qualities that are within all of us and that we tap into." It continued, stating these are "archetypes of higher, transpersonal forces" which are not always easily accessible to us. "Yoga has always offered practices for tuning in to these archetypal forces," it added. The article continued, stating that "tuning into…archetypal forces" is the first indicator that there are real forces and "powers" to be utilized. The article went on to say that the mantras recited in Yoga practice are "a means of tapping into deity

---

[29] Churchofsatan.com/faq-ritual-and-ceremony.
[30] Churchofsatan.com/satanic-youth-communique.

energy," energies which bring protection, prosperity, and inspiration. "Invoking deity energy is a way of opening yourself to energies within that can support, protect, and act with a kind of numinous power," it added. Importantly, *numinous* is defined as "having a strong religious or spiritual quality; indicating or suggesting the presence of a divinity." Take note: *the presence of a divinity*. This is not an archetype anymore.[31]

---

[31] *Yoga Journal*, "How to Be Fierce," October 17, 2008.

Chapter Ten

The Story of the Transformation of the Daughter of Anton LaVey

The life of Zeena Schreck is fascinating, particularly her departure from Satanism, which was driven by her profound change of perspective. Born Zeena LaVey, she is the daughter of Anton LaVey, the man who launched the infamous Church of Satan. Zeena renounced the surname LaVey and now only accepts "Schreck", the latter being the surname of her former husband Nikolas.[1] Since she and Nikolas shared a similar vision of the world, their comments are placed alongside each other in this section, and the story of each of their transformations will be told together.

In 1989, in their first interview with Bob Larson, Nikolas Schreck was adamant that they did not believe in demons. "I don't believe in demons," Nikolas said. "It's a mythical word. 'Incubus,' it's an archetype. It is a real force. *You* believe in demons," he said to Larson, "I don't." Satan, they explained, is no more real than they saw Christ to be. Satan is an archetype, the god of the strong and powerful and the leaders of the world. "No God, no devil. Just us, as animals?" Larson clarified. "That's what it boils down to, yeah," Zeena confirmed.

By 1997, their beliefs had markedly changed. Zeena and Nikolas had left the Church of Satan and become "Setians" in the Temple of Set. In their second interview with Larson, which took place after this change, they stated that "Satanist" is an outdated term and "Setian" is preferable. *Set* is the most ancient god known to the

---

[1] As will be discussed, Zeena renounced her father's Church of Satan and said, among other things, that she and all others were "suckers" who were "conned" by LaVey. She also said she had been "lied to since childhood" about what the Church of Satan really was. [Interview with Nikolas and Zeena Schreck from *Obskure Magazine* by Maxime Lachaud, September 2011] Further, her husband, Nikolas Schreck, said the *Satanic Bible* was a "paperback exploitation thing to cash in on *Rosemary's Baby*." [See below]

human race, they claimed. Egyptians saw him as the "lord of darkness." Set was the ruling god of Egypt when the Israelites were there. Zeena and Nikolas stated they are not "followers" of Set, since Setianism is a *left-hand path* religion. "We do not worship the devil, we use the archetypal figure, Set, as a prototype, a role model, a companion. He is literal – he is an entity," Zeena added.[2]

When Larson pressed them on whether they fraternize with demons, Nikolas eventually stated, "As black magicians, we look upon the powers of darkness as our friends, as peers; we do not worship them; they don't control us." Zeena added, "Nor do we view them as particularly interested with our outcomes, as your Jehovah would be."[3] Here, they reveal a significant change in their beliefs from just eight years prior when they were in the Church of Satan.

In 2011, Zeena said that her departure from the Church of Satan, and her renunciation of her last name and of her association with her father and the LaVey family, was due to her realization that she and everyone else, except the founder, Anton LaVey, and his mistress, were being duped and conned and the whole thing was the invention of a charlatan.[4] In 2012, she stated that, after she *reluctantly* joined "another group," the Temple of Set, she was sad to realize it was very similar to the Church of Satan. The group was "an Anton LaVey fan club," she said. "It was my father's legacy, another abusive and corruptive group, and not at all what I was interested in."[5]

That same year, 2012, Nikolas revealed how much he was still evolving in his own beliefs about Satanism. He also admitted to what he actually believed in 1989, contradicting the statements he had given at that time in his interview with Bob Larson. He said, "I've renounced a great deal of what I said and believed in that early period. In the late '80s, I was an arrogant and vengeful blood-drinking theistic devil worshipper.[6] After some misguided wandering through the more confused depths of organized occultism, we

---

[2] Note that, here, they state that Set is *both* an archetype *and* a companion, a real entity.
[3] This is an important admission. It mirrors what former occultists have stated, having encountered this disinterest from the demons in the form of abuse and attacks.
[4] *Obsküre Magazine*, September 2011, "Interview with Nikolas and Zeena Schreck" by Maxime Lachaud. Accessed via Zeena.eu, via archive.org.
[5] *Vice.com*, September 25, 2012, "Beelzebub's Daughter."
[6] Another important admission. With Larson in 1989, he presented it all as psychological, and that demons are not real, but by 2012 he was saying that he was in fact a devil worshipper at the time, a term that is used by theistic Satanists to be understood literally.

founded the Sethian Liberation Movement in 2002. Slowly but surely, over many years, that led us to formally convert to the left-hand path of Tantric Buddhism, which is centered on generating the universal compassion we used to disdain and dissolving the very ego we used to glorify. That doesn't mean that I now deny the existence of the devil, by whatever name you prefer to call him. But now he's more like an old friend I don't have much reason to keep in touch with anymore."[7]

The same Zeena who appeared cold and without compassion in her 1989 interview with Bob Larson,[8] eventually founded a group called *Phoenix* that helps people resolve painful issues through Eastern meditation and spiritual guidance. She worked with drug addicts, child stars, and former members of cults (Scientology, Jehovah's Witness, etc.), helping them "in overcoming their problems the same way I did."[9] While this effort is based within a pagan religion, it is a sign that a love of her neighbor had emerged from beneath the shroud with which Satanism had suffocated it.

Renouncing Satanism

On her own website, under the name Zeena Schreck, which, as of this writing, was last updated in April of 2022, she stated very clearly, and strongly, that she has renounced Satanism, all hierarchical esoteric groups and practices, and western occult trends. Her website stated, "Her reasons for this disavowal are due to her own life's experience witnessing how and why such pseudo-religious, occult or otherwise hierarchical esoteric groups and practices are not a viable route to freedom, liberation and enlightenment. Her first-hand experience in such groups proved to her that they are traps, often leading to worse manipulation, abuse, exploitation, mental and physical suffering and decay than conventional religions."[10]

The website also stated, "It should be noted that Zeena renounced all forms of Satanism and has not been a Satanist for over 30 years." It added that she believes "LaVeyan Satanist behavior in

---

[7] *Obsküre Magazine*, September 2011, "Interview with Nikolas and Zeena Schreck" by Maxime Lachaud. Accessed via Zeena.eu, via Archive.org.
[8] Larson video #1.
[9] *Vice.com*, September 25, 2012, "Beelzebub's Daughter."
[10] Zeenaschreck.com/general-info.html.

practice is best understood as 'Dark Triad personality disorder' with cosplay and ritual fetishes." This personality disorder is a combination of Machiavellianism, narcissism, and psychopathy, each of which are considered to contain malevolent qualities.

Nikolas Schreck has also recently spoken out against Satanism and in very strong terms. He not only condemned Satanism, but he also condemned invoking Satan's name and any symbolism associated with him, giving a warning that associating yourself with Satan invites a malevolent energy into your life. In a video interview in January 2022, referring to the introduction to one of his books, Nikolas Schreck discussed just who and what Satan is, from his perspective and experience. He explained his reasoning for adding this clarification, stating, "I found it to be so necessary because there's so much misunderstanding about this topic, about 'What is Satan?', 'Who is Lucifer?', 'What is the devil?', because there's so many wrong assumptions." Highlighting that people only remember him for who he was in the 1980s and 1990s, he added, "If people don't look into it, they don't realize that there's probably nobody on earth who has renounced it with the ferocity and viciousness with which I have." Here, he is referring to Satanism, with which he was once deeply involved. "It is totally, totally worthless," he continued, "a dead end of no spiritual value and also completely misunderstood."[11]

Though he is not a Christian at this point, and his view of Satan is not perfectly in line with that of the Church, his warning must not be disregarded. He added, "The devil, Satan, Lucifer, is not what Satanists or Christians believe it to be. Of course, I have to address: it is a truly existent being. In no way do I think now, or have I ever thought, that it's just a symbol or a myth or a legend. It is an actual being and if you're going to have the arrogance to say you represent that being, you better damn well know who and what it is. Many people don't because they think it's just a game to play, but I can tell you from personal experience: *it's not a game* and it will have very malevolent results if you work with that power, with that energy,

---

[11] The Nikolas Schreck Channel. "Nikolas Schreck Interviewed by Legs McNeil THE DARK SIDE OF THE SIXTIES PT 2 HOLLYWOOD SATANISTS," *YouTube*, April 17, 2022.

without knowing what it is; and it's not what Christians think it is, it's not what Satanists think it is, for the most part."[12]

He continued, "Like any spiritual being, you cannot use the symbolism and name of any being, I don't care if it's Athena or Odin or Lucifer, without knowing exactly what are you conjuring, what are you bringing into your life. So, that's a very serious warning I want to add. So, if people assume somehow that I still have any sympathy for it, having seen the depths of the entire Satanic world, all of it, having known most of the people who are supposedly the leading lights and quotes of the Satanic world, and being totally disappointed and disenchanted by them, I absolutely don't recommend it as anything to get involved with at all."[13]

Coming from a former leading Satanist, the former son-in-law of Anton LaVey, in addition to the condemnations of Satanism Zeena herself has made, all Satanists and occultists alike should take heed. "It's not a game."

---

[12] Ibid. Here, Nikolas further admits that he has *always* believed that Satan was an actual being.
[13] Ibid.

Chapter Eleven

The Exorcism of a Satanic Priestess

I was reading about the case of a possessed woman, as recounted by Dr. Richard Gallagher, a psychiatrist who wrote the excellent book, *Demonic Foes,* in which he described his many years of working alongside exorcists, assisting them from a Catholic psychological perspective. As I read through the account, I was more strongly persuaded of one of the key reasons God allows such a thing as possession to occur: the temporal spiritual plight of a possessed person reveals what such a diabolical companionship will be like in eternity.[1]

A Case in Point

The possessed woman mentioned above was a self-proclaimed "high priestess" in a Satanic cult who had willingly pledged herself to Satan and to the cult and had enjoyed quite impressive preternatural powers as a result of her dedication to Satan and her cooperation in evil. For example, through the agency of evil spirits, as she demonstrated to Dr. Gallagher and to the exorcist, she was able to remotely stir animals to violence and was able to "see," from a distance of many miles, exactly what the exorcist was doing.

Eventually, she sought out the exorcist because she realized she was possessed and did not particularly enjoy this aspect of her Satanic involvement. Simply being a Satanist or being part of a cult does not bring about possession, but it does place one in a situation where extraordinary diabolical activity is highly likely, though not guaranteed. Despite her displeasure with the possession, this woman

---

[1] This was originally published as an article on *OnePeterFive* on November 11, 2021. It has been slightly modified for the present work.

was not yet willing to renounce her dedication to Satan. She simply wanted the *possession* to end.

Her level of commitment to ridding herself of the demon and the degree of her attachment to Satan and the cult were unclear throughout the process of working with the exorcist and the psychiatrist. As a result, or simply as an indicator of the strength of her bond with the demon, the exorcisms proved to be particularly challenging. As the exorcist recounted, after one of the exorcisms, because of the strength of the demon's resistance, and the preternatural manifestations in the room during the exorcism, he felt like he had been "at the gates of Hell." The manifestations included cries and groans and animal howlings, such that it felt like they were "in the middle of a dangerous jungle." The temperature in the room plummeted to freezing and then spiked to a degree of heat that made it feel as if they were standing next to a boiler. These manifestations are not uncommon in the experience of exorcists, though they are often indicative of a more powerful demon being present.

The Desire of the Will

This possessed woman had chosen to serve Satan, did so daily, and enjoyed many "benefits" in return. She was hooked, both in the corruption of her will and by the "claw" of Satan who was not willing to let her go. The feeling that she was unable to escape, which her bondage to Satan communicated, was partially real for the following reasons: 1) her free dedication of herself to Satan, 2) her repeated rituals involving grave evil (such as abortions) freely performed to honor this dedication, and 3) her use of preternatural gifts and assistance from evil spirits. At that point, she was not only hooked on the power and the promises and the "protection" that Satan provided – she was legally bound to Satan and unable to break free without the aid of Christ working through His Holy Church.

This is one of the important aspects of this case. The demons resisted the exorcist and based their resistance on the claim that "no one has a right to liberate her" because she had freely given herself to them. It is not uncommon for the demon to make this assertion, particularly when the root cause of the possession involved the individual freely inviting the demon inside of them. However, while the demon is correct that the person freely chose the possession, and that this made the bondage stronger, Christ and His Church still have the right and authority to liberate her. This claim by the demons reflects one of the torments with which demons afflict individuals: despair, resulting from the threat that *God cannot save them* since they freely chose this miserable state.

For her to break free, she needed to fully renounce Satan and all his empty promises, and dedicate herself to Jesus Christ, submitting to the liberating yoke of His Gospel and grace. When we renew our Baptismal promises, which is recommended by exorcists and traditionally done on the anniversary of our Baptism, we use this language: "I renounce Satan...and all his works...and all his empty show." She, however, did not want to do this, so the exorcism failed. She still wanted the company of the demons, the power from Satan, and the reward of serving him in Hell as his "queen," as she was regarded in her cult.

Through the Gates of Hell

Those in a state of mortal sin, who have refused or have broken from the easy yoke of the Gospel, are in a state of spiritual bondage to Satan at the moment of death. As a result of this, they are led captive into perdition and eternal suffering in Hell. This is how we are damned: by leaving the passing realm of this mortal life without the fortification of sanctifying grace. In a possession we see a glimpse of what Satan's kingdom will be like in its fullness: domination, despair, torture of the senses, and imprisonment to evil desires.

In my research, I have begun to realize that there are surprising permissions which God has granted to the diabolical once the demons are welcomed into the life of an individual. These permissions, these actions, are warnings to us all, for, essentially, they are what await us in Hell should we have the misfortune to end up there. In cases of possession, many experience being beaten by invisible entities, in such a way that real bruises are left on their bodies. They are also scratched and strangled. Further, many report being sexually assaulted at night by these same invisible entities. An additional experience, as reported by Dr. Gallagher, is that of an internal burning sensation caused by the demon who is tormenting them. This, of course, is in addition to a wide variety of other pains and apparent diseases which the demons can cause in the person's body.

The Satanist mentioned above spoke to the psychiatrist of experiencing punishments from Satan many times prior to her visits to the exorcist to end the possession. When they told her she needed to renounce Satan, she remarked that it was impossible, stating, "Renounce Satan! Are you kidding me? How can I do that? Who knows what'll happen to me? This isn't someone you want against you. Trust me, I know." She understood her own personal experience of the "burning sensation" to have been caused by Satan, whom she otherwise served willingly. This was just one aspect of the punishments he inflicted on her even while she "faithfully" served him for years. She expected, after her death, to be given a high place in his Kingdom in Hell, as she was promised, even though she expected this to also entail the experience of his punishments.

"As We Are, So You Will Be"

While the average faithful Catholic will not personally experience these extraordinary attacks from the diabolical, a knowledge of the abilities and motivations of demons is nonetheless critical. Not only in the experience of the possessed, but also in the experience of the great Saints, we see manifestations of the true malice of the diabolical. When confronted with a willing victim (as in possession) or a staunch opponent (as with the great Saints), demons are inclined to reveal their true identities, remove their masks, and "take the gloves off." The assaults that they wield reveal both their hatred for humanity, their total disgust for the sacred, and their natural ability to inflict harm on mankind. When God permits it, faced with a willing victim or a great Saint, demons will make it known exactly what they long to do to man when they are allowed to get their hands on him.

Thus, the existence of extraordinary diabolical activity serves to warn everyone, even those who never personally experience it, of one key spiritual truth: *Hell is truly Hell.* The same demons who, here on earth, depend on God's permission to attack us, will have a free hand in Hell to administer every form of torment they have conceived, with no one greater than them present to liberate those souls from their grasp.

Therefore, Pray and Fight Today

As faithful Catholics, we have no cause for fear. We have all the weapons and means of grace to fortify our souls and persevere in grace to the end...and be saved. Though repentance for sin out of a fear of Hell is called "imperfect contrition," it is, nonetheless, sufficient to obtain God's pardon in Confession, a Sacrament whose abundant graces often bring about powerful conversions in the lives of those previously living in sin. The desire to avoid Hell is a great motivator for sanctity and a frequent impetus to achieve it.

Let us all heed the teachings of exorcists and the stories of those who suffer under diabolical affliction. They offer much to instruct us as we navigate this world which currently shudders under a renewed onslaught of the powers of darkness. We must be like St. Teresa of Avila who, in her famous prayer, reminds us, "Let nothing disturb you, let nothing frighten you." It was this same Saint who, in the midst of frequent attacks from demons, took great consolation both in the power of holy water to repel them and the obvious limitations that Our Lord set upon their activity. We are sons of Light and temples of the Holy Spirit. We must remain that way, growing in grace and strength in the face of spiritual opposition. In time, if we are faithful, not only will we conquer the agents of darkness, but we will, in glory, on the Day of Judgment, participate in their condemnation. St. Paul asked the Christians of Corinth, "Know you not that we shall judge [fallen] angels?"[2] Thus, in this life as well, we must have no fear of them.

---

[2] 1 Cor 6:3 DR

Chapter Twelve

The Dangers of the Ouija Board

Though the Ouija board has proven to be an enduring means of spiritual thrills for curious youth, it truly is, as the Church has repeatedly warned, a dangerous instrument. Despite the fact that many look upon it as a mere game, exorcists, former occultists, and even *active* occultists, confirm that it is something to stay away from. A recurring theme uncovered by my research is the unpredictability of the power of the entities that occultists summon. Because of this, by occultists' own admission, many occult practices are quite dangerous.[1] This includes the Ouija board. Ignorance about this issue continues to lead countless souls into grave spiritual trouble.

The Ouija board was first advertised as a "talking board" in 1891 in Pittsburgh, by a shop that sold toys and novelty gifts. It appears to have first emerged in 1886, in Ohio, and became a tool of the popular Spiritualism movement. The Kennard Novelty Company was the first to create and market the board, giving it the name "Ouija." This name was initially thought to be an ancient Egyptian word for "good luck," but it is now regarded as simply a combination of the words "yes" in the French (*oui*) and German (*ja*) languages. The creators were also able to get a patent for the board after they successfully demonstrated that it "worked" during a visit to the patent office in DC. The patent did not discuss *how* the board worked and, it seems, the company that made the board had more concern for profits than it did for what was hiding behind the answer to that question.[2] The Ouija board was eventually bought by Parker

---

[1] See *The Rise of the Occult*, especially chapter Eleven.
[2] *Smithsonianmag.com*, October 27, 2013, "The Strange and Mysterious History of the Ouija Board."

Brothers in 1967, which then sold two million boards in the first year.[3]

The widespread fame and availability of the board has made it commonplace in the culture. The Ouija board was at the center of the true story of the possession of a young boy in 1949 which was the inspiration for the famous movie "The Exorcist." In the true story, a fourteen-year-old boy became possessed after using a Ouija board to contact his deceased aunt shortly after her death. It was this same aunt, a spiritualist, who had first introduced the boy to the Ouija board. After having recourse to the board, strange phenomena began in his house which eventually led to the boy becoming possessed.

Fr. Gregory, as a Catholic school chaplain, has found that the Ouija board remains very prevalent among young people. "They think it is simply a game and nothing more," he said. When he presented the seriousness of the Ouija board in the middle school, they were surprised, as if they did not know it was actually bad. When he taught this to students on the high school level, to those who had not been instructed about it while in middle school, the students responded indifferently and rejected the idea that the boards were evil. Father said he got a lot of pushback on that topic, and on witchcraft in general, on the high school level. "They just don't see how harmful it is," he said. However, the danger is clear. Fr. Alphonsus, an exorcist and Catholic school chaplain, once helped two girls, one Catholic and the other not, who got into trouble after playing with a Ouija board. "Suddenly, they started getting scratches at night and hearing noises in their room and all these other things that clearly were the demonic, and they were scared to death," he explained. "Thankfully, after doing simple deliverance prayers, everything stopped."

Some, who take up an interest in the Ouija board, do not lay it down easily. When Fr. Thomas was in college, there was a young man in his dorm building who had an ability to use the Ouija board very effectively. Others in his dorm would just play it out of curiosity, as if they were listening to a ghost story. No one had any sense of a moral prohibition against playing with it. It was a small campus, he said, so, when people were messing with it and it did not

---

[3] *Time.com*, October 21, 2016, *"Ouija: Origin of Evil* and the True History of the Ouija Board."

work, they would call in this guy. When he showed up and joined them, only one other person would put their hands on it with him. It would always move, each time, in a quick and steady fashion, in the shape of an eight,[4] almost like it was being run by a machine. When it would answer a question, it would break from that figure eight path and hit the spots on the board as needed. Father witnessed this himself and knew that there was no way the young man could have known anything about the topics and the questions being asked. "Everyone was spooked," he said, "and some would leave the room immediately."

A benign experience with a Ouija board seems to be the rarity. Fr. Ermatinger recounted the story of a high school boy who had a violent and persistent run-in with a demon after playing with a Ouija board and sought the help of a seminarian afterward. The boy was known to be a "tough guy" yet he, after playing with a Ouija board, came to the seminarian trembling in fear. The seminarian, now an exorcist, recounted the boy's personal testimony as follows: "For three weekends in a row my friends and I have been using a Ouija board every Saturday night. We lit a candle, turned out the lights, and invoked spirits to see if it would work. Of course, we were only curious at the beginning. But it worked from the get-go. Each time it was more responsive, and we felt more daring. This last Saturday was horrible. Someone said, 'If there is a spirit here, please tap each one of us on the shoulder.' It did not only tap on the shoulder but gave all of us a beating as if we were being punched and kicked and bit. I ran home as fast as I could, leaving my Ouija board in my friend's basement. When I got home, I threw myself on my bed, scared and crying. But when I went into my bathroom to wash my face, the Ouija board was laid out on my sink, ready to play."[5] Adelaide agreed on this last point. She has also heard that you can't get rid of the board after that. "It keeps coming back," she said.

Many former occultists testify to the danger of the Ouija board. Christopher referred to the Ouija board as the most obvious (and "stupidest") way to let a demon into your home. "Even Satanists

---

[4] Interestingly, the "Magic 8 Ball" has its origin in Spiritualism. It is the fifth version of a divination tool first created by a clairvoyant for use in communicating with "spirits." As far as my research concluded, there is no connection between this Ouija spirit and the Magic 8 Ball.

[5] Ermatinger, *Trouble with Magic*, 30.

don't use them," he added. He even avoids movies that present Ouija boards, seeing these movies as conduits of the same troubles as the actual boards. In his experience, the most common rituals for divination he has seen are tarot card and runes, not Ouija boards. "Most practitioners," he said, "have early experiences of some kind with a Ouija board that scares them to death." As a result, they see the Ouija board as a "toy for idiots to play with."

When Adelaide was a practicing witch, her witch friends strongly warned her against using a Ouija board. "I was told that if they [her two witch friends] ever heard about me touching a Ouija board, they would drop me like a bad habit," she said. "Witches know. You just don't touch those." The warning she had been given by these two women, one being her mother-in-law and the other her mother-in-law's witch friend, was related to an experience that the two of them had had when they were younger. The basic idea is, Adelaide said, "It would bring on something you cannot control." Apparently, they played with a Ouija board and whatever came into the house at that point almost killed one of them.[6] She is not certain of all the details but that is the origin of the warning they gave her. "They were very clear about not touching one," she said. In a separate story related to me, as recorded in *Slaying Dragons*, a dark shadowy being appeared to two kids when they were playing with the board. It appeared again the next day in the middle of a road, causing them to swerve off the road and crash, paralyzing one of them.[7] In response to hearing this story from me, and recalling what she has also heard, Adelaide said, "The dark shadowy figure is a common thing, and destruction often follows." When Gabriel was dabbling in the New Age, he said he held a belief in ghosts and demons and decided to stay away from Ouija boards. He was being taught that there were both good spirits and bad spirits and, with Ouija boards, you had to be careful because you never knew which spirit would respond.

---

[6] Recall, from *The Rise of the Occult*, Fred's experience in chapter Eleven and Christopher's in chapter Fifteen.

[7] Fraune, *Slaying Dragons*, 19.

Story: The Effects of a Ouija Board

Adelaide shared a story that explains one of the impacts of the demons that can enter someone's life through a Ouija board.[8] One of her children, Mark, was in middle school shortly after her initial yet lukewarm and very incomplete conversion. One weekend, Adelaide's mother took Mark to her "rather odd" Protestant community for a Sunday school lesson. It was Halloween weekend and the Sunday school teacher decided to bring in a Ouija board and direct the children on how to use it. One exorcist has stated that curiosity, very present among Protestants because of their ignorance of the Church's answers to questions about death, the afterlife, and the preternatural, leads some of them to try out these boards, which in the end prove to be very addictive. Later that day, Adelaide took Mark to join his brother, Augustine, at the youth group at the Catholic Church, which they had already joined at this point in her conversion. Augustine, she said, was there mainly for the social time with the other kids and not for the formation in the Faith.

In the car on the way, Mark told her about his encounter with the Ouija board. When they arrived at the Church, Adelaide was very disturbed. She went directly to the priest, "cornered him," as she described it, and told him what happened. She said, "I asked him to bless the boy and do whatever a priest is supposed to do." She was still very clueless about the Faith and did not really know what to say to him. The priest, she described, "Raised his hands, backed away and said, 'I don't do that'." This, she said, "disgusted me," which prompted her to begin attending a nearby parish that was much more traditional. Within days of the Ouija board incident, she said, "the whispers and footsteps that were already present in the house turned into actual physical attacks against Mark."[9] That boy had become the main target of the thing that had been following them from house to house during the many relocations Adelaide had resorted to in her attempt to escape what she thought was a demon haunting their home.[10] Before the board, it was just the footsteps,

---

[8] Mentioned in *The Rise of the Occult*, 340.
[9] For more about the diabolical retaliation she endured, see *The Rise of the Occult*, 244.
[10] As told in *The Rise of the Occult*, Adelaide eventually realized it was not the homes in which they lived but the occult associations of her past which had been bringing these diabolical attacks upon her family.

phantom cat, and shower turning on, among other things. After the Ouija board, the boy woke up twice with bloody claw marks down his back, the letter 'M' burned into the carpet, and something whispering the word 'Markus.'

After that, when she still thought it was the house that was the problem and not a demon following her, Mark's eye was spontaneously cut while walking down the hall, without any object coming in contact with him. Adelaide flushed the eye but couldn't see anything other than a little irritation. At first, Mark tried to ignore the discomfort, thinking it was nothing major, but then his eye began to swell shut so they took him to the ER. They checked his eye with a fluorescein eye stain and saw clearly that it had been cut from the very top of the eye to the very bottom; a thin slice all the way down. She said it was like the demon was alerting her, "I am here, and I can hurt you."

"Ouijazilla" – An American Occult Phenomenon

Calling the current cultural interest in the Ouija board an act of "curiosity" does not sufficiently describe it. An unbelievable story explains how deep the obsession with the Ouija board can go. In 2016, someone thought they had accomplished something remarkable by putting the "world's largest Ouija board" on top of a purportedly haunted hotel in Windber, Pennsylvania. This was deemed significant enough to be named the "Guinness World Record holder" for the largest Ouija board. However, in 2019, in honor of the current global descent into superstition, paganism, and the occult, someone in Salem, Massachusetts decided to build what is referred to as "Ouijazilla." This Ouija board is not on top of a hotel but in an open field and is large enough for five full-sized eighteen-wheelers to park on top of it.

In discussing the unveiling of Ouijazilla, a Boston news outlet provided an effective hook: "Whose spirit will be summoned with the help of the [sic] what's being touted as the world's largest Ouija board? Those visiting Salem on Saturday are about to find out."[11] But, as exorcists say, by the time you find out what spirit it is that

---

[11] *Boston.com*, October 11, 2019, "It's been called the world's largest Ouija board and it's about to descend on Salem."

you have just summoned, it's too late. For the Talking Board Historical Society, the group responsible for creating this monstrosity, apparently that is a risk they are willing to *encourage others* to take. In what is clearly another sign of the occultic corruption of Halloween, and the diabolical inversion of All Saints, Ouijazilla was unveiled that year just three weeks before the great Solemnity.

Ouijazilla's predecessor of infamy, the crown of the haunted hotel of Windber, had been unveiled close to All Saints in 2016, on October 28, just four days before the sacred Feast. From the fascinating article on this haunted hotel,[12] the reader can see that, while the hotel may have been trumped by Ouijazilla when it comes to the Guinness World Records, the hotel is still capably competing when it comes to preternatural manifestations. Blair Murphy, the mastermind behind the giant Ouija board on top of the hotel, spoke about the intensity of preternatural manifestations which characterized the hotel for a number of years. Eventually, years after he and his wife and daughter had moved into the hotel, the amount of activity dropped off almost entirely. The silence lasted for about two years. Missing the preternatural antics, they decided to play with a Ouija board inside the hotel, hoping to stir up the spirits. The impact of that moment was remarkable. As the article says, "According to the independent movie maker [Murphy], the results were terrifying." The article continued, saying,

> "Things flipped out throughout the hotel. Energies were swirling. Guests were getting completely freaked out," says Blair, "it seemed to kick things up into an entire new level of paranormal activity. We were seeing floating people and hearing voices and even the hotel pets were flipping out and reacting to unseen forces. Our dreams were pretty wild. And it wasn't just us. Other longer-term hotel residents were saying 'there is absolutely something going on here' and having their own middle of the night weird encounters."[13]

---

[12] *Guinness World Records*, January 23, 2017, "Haunted hotel is now home to the world's largest Ouija board."
[13] Ibid.

That gave them an idea: a giant Ouija board *on top* of the hotel would make sure the demons knew they were completely welcome in the building. So, they built one, completing it in 2016. In the article, Murphy spoke about sensing the hotel calling him to live there. "I always looked at it like the hotel chose me," he said.[14] Interestingly, William Fuld, who worked for the Kennard Novelty Company, the original creators of the board, told the *Baltimore Sun* in 1919 that the Ouija board had told him specifically to build his Hartford Avenue factory. This factory would come to be the sight of his accidental death, when a railing at the factory gave way and he fell from the roof of the structure.[15]

Modern Manifestations of Ouija: "Charlie, Charlie"

Today, the Ouija spirit is emerging in a variety of manifestations.[16] One of the clearest examples is that of the ever-increasingly common childhood "game" called "Charlie, Charlie." This game involves balancing one pencil on top of another over a piece of paper with "yes" and "no" written on it. The children then call upon "Charlie, Charlie," with a rhyming incantation and then ask it questions. The game is notorious, like the Ouija board, for giving occultic responses.

One teacher with whom I spoke told me, "I was working in a school, about six or seven years ago, with elementary students. During recess, they would play a game called 'Charlie, Charlie' to summon an evil spirit. They had no idea how bad it was. It's like that *bloody Mary* thing where you look in the mirror in the dark. Both are dangerous and most of the kids had no clue. I warned them, even though it was a public-school setting." This game has proven to be quite dangerous and, essentially, it is no different from a Ouija board.

Marianne, a Catholic mother, told me about a conversation with her daughter after she learned that *Charlie Charlie* was played by kids at her daughter's school. This is a good example of how to speak to your children about the occult practices which might cross their paths in this age of the world. Here is her account:

---

[14] Ibid.

[15] *Baltimore Magazine*, October 25, 2020, "Not Dead Yet" also "The Dark History Behind Ouija Boards."

[16] See chapter Fifteen for yet another example: "ghost-hunting apps"

The Dangers of the Ouija Board

I casually asked Matilda, a very articulate 4-year-old, "Have you ever played a game called *Charlie Charlie?*" She answered, "No." I didn't want to make a big deal out of it so I told her to please let me know if she ever did, and I thought that would be the end of it.

A short time later, she dutifully reported that some other kids were playing. I contacted the daycare and advised that this game was not appropriate for small children in any circumstance, and, on top of that, spiritually unsettling at best.

I carefully crafted my best four-year-old explanation of why I didn't want her to join this "game." I tried to ask more questions than to speak at her, not wanting to make it scary. "So," I said, "in the game we ask someone named Charlie to move the pencils around. Do you think there is really someone named Charlie moving the pencils?" "No," Matilda replied, "it's probably the wind or the person holding them." "I think you're probably right," I responded, adding, "But what if someone named Charlie *did* come move the pencils? How do we know who Charlie is?" "I don't know," Matilda said.

"So, if we don't know who Charlie is, is it smart to invite Charlie to play with us? What if Charlie isn't really our friend?" I said. "Oh, that would be bad," said Matilda. "Do you think the devil is clever?" I replied. "Yes," said Matilda. I then added, "Do you think he could disguise himself as your friend and call himself Charlie?" At this, Matilda's eyes got big. *Maybe I took it too far*, I thought. Looking ahead, eight years later, I don't think so. So, I concluded that conversation, saying, "So even though we are pretty sure there is no Charlie and it is just a silly game, we never, ever want to invite someone we don't know to play with us, because it's not safe."

Recently, within the past month or two even, Matilda, now 12, came to me about something. "Remember that game from a long time ago? It was like, a boy's name twice, and it started with a C," she said. "Yes, I remember," I responded. "Well," Matilda explained, "I overheard some kids playing a game that seemed kinda like it, and I was really glad that those kids aren't really my friends. We don't do stuff like that."

Even though I'm socially and spiritually rather conservative, my approach to communication and openness about worldly issues has been rather progressive and open. I can only pray that God guides each of us as parents to communicate in the way that leads our children closer to God, into open communication with parents, and instills a sense of awe for beautiful things and healthy suspicion toward the unfamiliar without losing a sense of exploration and wonder.

Attentive, thoughtful counsel from a mother, whose virtue and faith are strong, really can help a child navigate the occultic storms that are brewing today.

Chapter Thirteen

The Lord Liberates, The Liar Oppresses

Our Lord desires for us a faith that produces holiness and good works. This enrages Satan, who persists in trying to undermine faith and to twist and pervert what is good and holy. He seeks to ruin every good that God has bestowed upon the world. Satan is the ape of God, as it is said, in that he mocks all that God does and offers counterfeit goods in place of what Our Lord is seeking to bestow upon us.[1]

God offers us glory if we follow Him. Satan does as well, but Satan's glory is of this world alone, which fades and ends in misery and disillusionment. The glory that Our Lord offers is eternal and must be awaited with great patience.

God offers power and strength and joy. Satan does as well, but his power is for our earthly gain, his strength is for us to persevere unchallenged in sin and evil, and his "joy" takes the form of earthly and obsessive pleasures which weaken and imprison us. The power and strength granted by Our Lord enable us to tread upon serpents, to patiently endure our sufferings, and to persevere in holiness against all obstacles. Our Lord's joy is from a supernatural vision of what fulfills us and secures our life in grace and goodness, with the hope of one day seeing the all-good God and Creator with our own eyes.

God offers us companionship and relationships. Satan does as well, but his companionship is abusive and threatening, and the relationships he delivers are with those who love evil and will only treat us as useful tools for their own pleasure and personal gain. Our Lord offers us companionship with the citizens of Heaven, who selflessly seek our good at all times, and relationships with His followers on earth, who likewise seek to be holy as He is holy.

---

[1] This was originally published as an article on *OnePeterFive*, January 10th, 2022.

God is truthful, and He delivers on His promises, constantly leading us forward in holiness and happiness. Satan is a liar and, if he does grant what he offers, he does so with the plan to use that "gift" against us to compel us to serve him in evil and die in mortal sin.

A Providential Conversation

It might seem to be a petty thing to some, but to those of faith and to those who have experienced Our Lord's coordination of events in their own lives, the following story will be edifying. It concerns the Providential juxtaposition of the liberating power of God against the oppressive goal of the Enemy.

Therese, a former occultist, when she was deep into her occult practice, summoned a specific demon to enter her house and dwell there. It seemed to her that this was an important moment in her ritual practices; from her perspective as a seasoned occultist, this summoning was not an extreme practice or something unheard of for her to attempt. However, as she finished this summoning ritual, her entire house began to groan and creak as if some great weight had come down upon it. It was clear to Therese that the demon had responded. It was also clear to her that she had made a big mistake.

At that moment in our conversation, which took place in the evening, I related to her something that had Providentially happened to me earlier *that very day*. I had attended Mass at mid-day in my parish Church. The Church is a tall wooden structure, and the roof often creaks and pops as the sun heats it up in the course of the day. However, this day, the day of my conversation with Therese, the creaking and popping was very different: it happened only once, very loudly, and at the precise moment of the first Consecration. Further, when this happened, which was several hours before hearing Therese's story, my initial thought was that it seemed like the whole roof wanted to lift off of the Church and open up to the sky like a flower, eager to receive the Lord of Hosts as He descended upon the altar. In the moment, I saw these sounds as a rather natural occurrence which Our Lord used to communicate to me a supernatural joy, and His timing for doing so was, as it turned out, very intentional.

The juxtaposition of my experience with Therese's recounting of her own is not only remarkable but educational:

- An occultist summons a demon and the house groans in agony at the crushing weight of its arrival, striking fear and anxiety in the hearts of the inhabitants.
- A Catholic priest brings Our Lord Jesus Christ into the Church through the power of the Holy Spirit and the Consecration of the Host, and the whole Church creaks and pops as if the building itself wished to embrace the Almighty with open arms. Inside, the faithful are filled with hope and joy and experience a surge of faith before the presence of God in their midst.

The Victorious Battle Makes the Sun Shine Brighter

When Our Lord entered the world, He initiated a real and often violent battle with the forces of evil. After His Birth, the devil orchestrated the slaughter of the Innocents whom the wicked King Herod thought could possibly be the newborn King Himself. When Our Lord manifested Himself in the midst of the people of Israel and began His public ministry, the devil sought to orchestrate His death at every turn until, at last, through the evil Roman empire, he accomplished this feat.

When we follow Our Lord in this world overrun by evil and under the power and influence of the Evil One, and we encounter the opposition which Satan wields against us, we are often prone to discouragement. He is crafty and convincing and very capable of leading us astray. We grow weary from his temptations and from laboring in the work of perseverance, often turning inward and relying upon ourselves alone for the strength to carry on. This weariness places us beneath Satan's oppressive works. If we would, instead, refuse to lay down the sword of faith and would choose to wield *this* weapon rather than our own fallen wills, we would remain as steadfast soldiers on the battlefield and, despite the injuries we may endure, would stand up in glory on the Day the dust settles.

Our Lord liberates us but Satan, the Liar, oppresses us. On the battlefield of salvation, the sun is indeed darkened, but it shines, nonetheless. When we hold fast to the Lord, the Satanic veil over this world will be pierced by His divine grace, and we will know, with the confidence found only in the Holy Spirit, that goodness will prevail despite the apparent strength of evil. The "weakness" of the martyr, who must let his life be snuffed out in this world, will be seen to be a divine strength, ushering him into the Kingdom of Heaven amidst fitting praise for his victory. When the victory is finally won for all followers of Christ, and Satan's mechanisms and instruments of deception are overthrown, the sun will shine all the brighter for the time it was veiled. Let us see the devil for who he is, resist him, and await, with hope and eager expectation, the glory of Christ's eternal victory.

Chapter Fourteen

Witchcraft and the Online World

As we all know, people can now find anything on the internet. Unfortunately for today's lost world, this includes practically everything in the realm of witchcraft and the occult. "The internet has led to a magnification of dabbling in the occult," Fr. Sebastian said. The prominence of the occult on television, such as ghost hunting shows, has greatly contributed to this. There are also apps, he said, that people can download to their phones that are used for ghost hunting and communicating with spirits.[1] "It draws them in," Father said, "and leads to the curiosity[2] part of it. It seduces them and then they take the next steps. The internet is the greatest in-road to the occult today. Before," he added, "you had to use real books and boards and cards but now, with the internet, everything is there. You're curious, you start clicking, and you get into it." He gets calls often from concerned parents, in particular about occult items on the internet. Kids today are getting started there, he emphasized.

This is confirmed by the world itself. According to a 2018 article on Allure.com, "With social media, it's easier than ever to discover the occult. In the past, most people learned about witchcraft through a family connection…[but] as social media made us more connected, access to information about subcultures of all kinds proliferated. Now, witches of Instagram are stepping into the spotlight not just as teachers and healers, but as lifestyle gurus."[3] The witch Lola said, "I spend a lot of my time on forums. I do meet a lot of people in real life that are practitioners, and I have a good deal of conversations with them. But online is where you find most of the communities and it is where a lot of practitioners go to bounce ideas off people and to

---

[1] See chapter Fifteen for an analysis of this reality.
[2] According to St. Thomas Aquinas, *curiositas*, knowledge pursued with bad motives, is a vice.
[3] *Allure.com*, December 26, 2018, "Astrology Offered Comfort in a Chaotic World."

discuss topics." One of these online resources for witches is on *Amino*, which offers lots of different witchcraft communities for people to join.[4] This is in addition to online witchcraft websites and forums, and the countless videos available online.

Andrew's own descent into the occult was initiated by what he was able to learn through the internet. He was brought up in a non-denominational Protestant home with a charismatic leaning. He fell away from this when he was a teenager and entered a religious "limbo" period. He became an atheist for several years and was unconvinced of the existence of the supernatural. An interest in the paranormal, however, began to emerge and, with the abundance of information on the internet, he felt that it was inevitable that this curiosity would lead him into the occult. He said that blogs, teenage rebellion, and a "resentment for my upbringing," led him to an interest in Satanism and demonology, eventually identifying with Luciferianism. "This," he said, "led to me reading as much about the occult as I could. I also began experimenting with psychedelics during this period in my life in an effort to 'unlock' secrets not only about my own consciousness but also about reality at large."

The isolation that resulted from the shutdown of society throughout the world in response to Covid has, according to Fr. Blaise, shown itself to be demonic in part because of the resulting dependence on the internet, and the evils that reside there, which it fomented. The reason behind this is that it left kids alone, online, and exposed to all sorts of evil, including everything about the occult. Many young people have gone deep into the occult quickly as a result. John agreed on this last point and added a warning that, when young Catholic kids go astray today and "dabble" in the occult, it won't be as simple as it was a few decades ago; it will become a full-blown exit from Christianity and a full move into the occult. This is due to the convergence of many influences: the internet, the spiritual vacuum in the culture, widespread faithlessness, immorality, broken families, a desire for instant gratification, materialism, media manipulation, and a prevailing new world order of Satanic philosophies and morals.

---

[4] Aminoapps.com; search for "pagans and witches" and other similar keywords to find the communities and see how large they can be.

Dr. Luke has observed that part of the problem today is that young people are craving attention and seeking to know that they have value, but they are seeking it in all the wrong ways: through social media. The way social media is working is simply to feed the loneliness and the sadness. Together on social media, though not united in any true way, the youth feed each other's sadness through these interactions. Satan is ready to jump on that sadness. Dr. Luke said they are also trying to stand out and feel special by adopting destructive lifestyles or labels, like being "bi-sexual" or claiming to be suicidal.

Story: The Destructive Power of the Internet

As the Becketts observed the decline of their daughter, Catherine, into the occult, the mother commented that the biggest source of destruction was the internet. The daughter was always on her phone. She was twenty-one at that point and, then living at the parents' home, she shared a room with the older sister, who was temporarily living at home as well. The older sister would notice that Catherine would still be on her phone even at three A.M. There was a constant glow from her corner of the room. She would also be drinking and vaping through the night.

As her mother told me, "It's not 'just Yoga' or 'just mindfulness.' All of her problems *started* with mindfulness." It went from mindfulness to crystals and candles. The candles, as Catherine admitted, were supposed to impart blessings of prosperity, money, and protection. When the mom asked her, "So, how did all of that work out for you?", Catherine was never able to give her an answer. As the mom said, Catherine has only gone downhill since getting into it. In addition to the occult, she also joined BLM, Antifa, another Communist group, and trans-supporting groups. "She used to be very patriotic," her father added.

The mother thinks the biggest thing that influenced her daughter toward the occult, or kept her stuck in it, "is these phones they all have." The daughter was always on the phone, always curious about mindfulness. She would talk about "people" offering her advice about mindfulness but, as the mother noted, she never left the house so it was only people she encountered online. She would stay up all night in chat groups with her "friends." The mom counseled her that these are not real friends and that she must not depend on these people as if they were. "They can't actually help her, locked away in the virtual world, so she must stop depending on them as friends," she explained.

Chapter Fifteen

The Phone Becomes the Voice of Satan: Spirit Summoning Apps

My research for this book led me down numerous trails of thought on the issues concerning the prevalence of the occult in our present culture. At one point, as I was processing the notes from one of my interviews with an exorcist, I recalled that he had mentioned the existence of "ghost hunting" apps. So, I decided to look into it.

Unexpected Results

My research for the specific kind of app he had mentioned quickly revealed a large number of apps that offered the same thing. The details contained below are only from looking at the Google Play store apps. I found this store easier to navigate than Apple, but we can presume that a search of the Apple store will provide the same insights. These apps are no trivial matter. My initial research turned up at least 15-20 of these apps: an impressive number. Then, after looking further, I found a better way to filter the results. The number of apps of this kind then jumped tenfold – approximately 150 different apps that enable you to "speak to spirits." However, I adjusted the search filter a third time and found almost 250! Some apps are old, others have fewer reviews, but nonetheless – 250!

Further, the number of reviews is indicative of how widespread the use of these apps might be. Some apps have less than a hundred, others a few hundred, others a few thousand, and then a few have tens of thousands of reviews. To be fair, this number often reflects whether the app is free or not, but nonetheless, people are using them and actively engaged in finding the one that works the best.

The Inherent Danger

Below, I have pulled together some reviews that people wrote for a few of the apps. In my searching, there were many people who left reviews saying these apps were fake, but many others who said they worked. Both of these statements are alarming. The people who said these apps were fake did so because they did not find them to be effective in their own efforts of *finding ghosts and talking to spirits,* which was their intent. *That is a problem in itself.* The others, for whom it did work, successfully communicated with "the dead" or "spirits," i.e., demons, and are going to suffer for it at some point and to some extent.

Even if these apps are fake or ineffective at detecting the presence of an invisible entity, the fact is that Attempting to communicate with spirits is objectively morally evil and makes one vulnerable to every sort of diabolical influence and attack, depending on God's permissions and other spiritual aspects. Further, we know from exorcists that demons will use technology to communicate and to harass people. They will surely, then, take advantage even of bogus "ghost" apps just as they take advantage of the cardboard, plastic, and ink of a Ouija board, or the pencil and paper of the "Charlie, Charlie" game. These mechanisms are simply the means by which an individual expresses his *will* to communicate with spirits. That is gravely evil...and always dangerous.

How People are Using the Apps to Encounter Spirits

I first focused on an app called "Necrophonic." Reviews for other apps were very similar, so this one should be indicative of the rest as well. As of my survey, this app had 4.1 out of five stars and 2,348 mostly positive reviews. Below, I chose to *italicize* certain words to emphasize the main problematic statements, but I have not otherwise altered the reviews, i.e., for grammar or spelling. One of the five-star reviewers highlighted one of the many evils of this "toy" in her review:

> I got *intelligent responses literally immediately.* I found a work around when it comes to the app not having a record option. You can use the audio recorder on the

computer or phone you're using for the app and the recordings are clear and audible. *I can't wait to use this app with my daughter!*

"With my daughter."

Another reviewer pointed out that the user will want to "meditate" before using the app, record their session, and go back and listen again. The reviewer did this, taking notes along the way, and was shocked by how much "communication" there was during the session. Proving my point above, another review said:

> The good news is, *spirits will readily use necrophonic* and you can get some good results with a little patience and concentrated *intent* between the user and the spirit.

As I will mention later, this app encourages people to continue in their occultic practices. Here is an important commentator, a five-star reviewer:

> I never rate anything on here but this app is something special. *I'm a medium* and this is absolutely the best tool for me to *verify who is coming through* and what their intentions are. One would think that the play store couldn't possibly produce *real paranormal communication tools* but this one delivers.

Other reviewers of Necrophonic said:
- Absolutely brilliant for *communicating with the other side.* Great for ghost hunting too. brilliant work.
- This app worked fantastic! With patience and learning you can *literally have full on intelligent conversations with spirits.* I was skeptical about the app at first but right now its the best in the business.
- This app is intense! It's not a toy or game either. It's a *well planned strait-forward tool to communicate to spirits,* I hear different male and female voices with certain dialect depending on where you live. This app knows me by name on many occasions.

- Awesome. This is awesome and *is helping my friend who passed over come through* ..she has said all our names and even the cats name to confirm its her..Love this app!![1]
- Okey dokey SO! I purchased and downloaded this tonight, *spoke with 3 different spirits* but spoke with the 3rd one twice . Recorded the sessions. But I must say the 2nd session was much more responsive to my specific questions being asked. *Cold chills each time.*[2]

An Encouragement to Evil

As should be evident at this point, these apps are tools that inflame a sinful curiosity about paranormal, preternatural, and supernatural phenomena. They encourage people who are mediums to continue in their practice, give "evidence" to those who think they have spirits around them, empower people to feel they can communicate with the dead on their own, and generally foster a spiritual attitude contrary to that revealed by God and taught by Him as holy and appropriate. One more example will serve to illustrate this point. A reviewer for a different app had this to say:

> Spot on Within a few minutes of activating *two voices came through.* One female and another male. Gave me goosebumps. I've always had a feeling we had guests in our home, now its confirmed. *In case, I'm burning sage and saying a prayer before bed.* This is cool app!

This individual is evidently lost in an occultic mindset and likely doesn't even know it. Not only was she suspicious that she had spirits living in her home, but she was also summoning them and others through this app. Further, ignorant as she already was, she was "burning sage" as a way of protecting herself before she went to bed. Sage burning (or sage smudging, as it is also called) is an occultic practice that can easily lead to diabolical harassment, such as home infestations, and further diabolical activity in the person's life.

---

[1] This specific review is from a different but similar app.
[2] This specific review is also from yet a third similar app.

Through this app, she is compounding the evil and will inevitably suffer for it.

Occultists Admit to the Danger of the Occult

As has been explained in this book and in *The Rise of the Occult*, occultists admit quite readily that there are dangers in the occult. New-Agers, Satanists, and witches all talk about certain things they will never do because the spirits that emerge from certain rituals are dangerous and uncontrollable. This danger is seen in the reviews for these apps as well. It is a theme within the occult that, I would guess, few are aware of, especially among those who are dabbling. Thankfully, a few reviewers expressed this caution, illustrating my point:

- This is not an app to mess with *it's very serious just don't be stupid with the app*
- Im a spirtual person and used this to contact my family. *always ask for protection* from your spirit guides before using this app also, *they are bad things out there.*
- So finally one that works... But maybe a little too well.. you *need an 18 and up notice for the app.. not all spirits are nice.* And the fact someone could find something they weren't looking for because there novice in this department *could leave them in trouble..* but it works.. man does it work. Not everyone can just talk to spirits.. there either drawn to you or there not...

For another product, "Echovox," with 1,175 mostly positive reviews, one review stated:

Listen very closely. This app is 1000% real and is different than all other spirit box apps. Not saying all *other spirit box apps* don't work because some do but echovox delivers straight intelligent responses and is *the most intelligent spirit box app* ever produced. I have gotten different spirits in different locations. *I have encountered demons on this app as_well.* If you do just ignore them and turn app off for a couple hours and restart. *This is not a toy. Be careful have fun...*

"There are demons here – have fun."

The Dangers are Multifaceted

For those who are alert to the presence of the occult in the culture, it is not difficult to say that the problem is worse than we all think. In an age where most people, and almost all youth, are left without spiritual guidance, all mankind seems to be "plugged in" to a "system" of some sort which is pumping evil into our minds in many forms and through many channels. Awareness is the first step. If there are people in your life, especially youth and parents of young children, use this knowledge to counsel them. Be observant and inquisitive. From what I have learned, most people are unaware of the existence and dangers of these channels of evil.

Chapter Sixteen

Reiki in the Wild

A specific form of occultic practice known as Reiki purports to manipulate the energies in a person's body and in "the Universe" in order to bring about healing and enlightenment. This practice has been condemned by the Church and is extremely dangerous. It also appears in other forms not under the same name. Reiki, like the rest of the occult, is popping up in unexpected places. It is important for people to be aware that practitioners of this occultic art have been seen to be aggressive and pushy about "sharing" this occultic "energy" with others.

Story: Reiki Interferes with a Holy Death

When Anna's mother was near death, the wayward nuns in their area were big practitioners of Reiki. At her mother's deathbed, one of the nuns wanted to do a Reiki healing over her mother. Anna's father, she explained, "Not wanting to hurt their feelings, permitted it!" As she said, "Things went downhill fast. [My mother] got an unusual growl in her voice and a glare of a look, from a woman who was never like that, staring at me while I was reading a book." The mother suddenly changed and developed a new and enduring negative attitude. They called the local priests for assistance and decided that the priests would offer Mass and, at the same time, Anna would stay with her mother and pray the Rosary, with everyone having the same intention of eradicating this evil. Her mother eventually joined in with that Rosary but with a very odd voice. In the end, her mother died well, Anna said, with the Sacraments and at peace, but there clearly seemed to be a battle for her mother's soul as death approached, likely initiated by the occult practice her husband permitted to take place.

Story: Coercion to Embrace Reiki during Labor

One mother shared this rather frightening story, which all women need to hear. Since this happened in the last ten years, the likelihood of it occurring at the typical hospital in the future is only going to increase.[1]

> During the birth of one of my children I was offered Reiki for pain control since I was not an epidural candidate. I had been open about my fear of handling the pain after a prior difficult labor. The doctor suggested Reiki and I declined after she described it as "channeling energies of the universe to come help you." She was from an Asian culture, and she reassured me that in her culture it was commonplace, though unfamiliar to Americans (at that time). After she left, the nurse also told me that I should try it because "it really works." During the most difficult point in labor, in my most vulnerable moment, they offered it to me again. I declined again and asked instead for a crucifix which I held throughout my delivery. I hate to think of the suffering my child would have had in life if I had allowed demons to be invoked for my personal comfort and they had preyed on *her*, or worse. I have a photo right after her birth, when they placed her on my lap, still with blood and vernix on her, and the photo shows the crucifix still in my left hand. Thank you, Jesus, for giving me the insight at that moment, when I wasn't entirely clear what Reiki was, to be repulsed by it. I'm sure my guardian angel, and that of my child, were the reason I was able to say a resolute "No," three times.

This story highlights what one exorcist stated, which was that the deities/spirits of all the cultures which are mixed into the American society, by immigrants from those cultures, are now present among us. Priests often see this, even among Catholics from

---

[1] Read about just some of the statistics of Reiki's spread in *The Rise of the Occult*, p. 40.

other cultures. These people have brought some of the idolatrous or superstitious practices of their homelands with them and invoke those spirits here in the States. This often causes spiritual problems for the pagan families themselves but, as this story illustrated, it also gives the opportunity for those spirits to negatively influence others as well. Regarding the above story about Reiki, Camilla added a warning, stating, "Lots of nurses in the country are trained in 'healing touch,' which is clearly another occult technique."[2]

Story: Pressured to Receive "Energy"

Reflecting the disturbing intrusiveness of Reiki in the story above, the following account, and the detail at the end by a former occultist, sheds even more light on this phenomenon. A person I met in my travels contacted me two weeks after my visit to her parish. She told me a fascinating and disturbing story that happened in the days following my visit.

> I walked into work this morning, thinking the door was locked behind me after I came in. Apparently, it got stuck halfway and the next thing I knew I was walking out from my cubicle and there was a strange guy here. I didn't hear him come in. He asked me about what we do and then asked if he could "pass energy" to me. He said this energy is "special" and is close to God. I immediately had a very bad feeling in the pit of my stomach. I told him to come back later. I immediately went to grab my holy medals (St. Benedict and St. Michael the Archangel) and let my colleague know before he left the office. The man came back and I tried to ask him his name and other things about him but he refused to answer me. He just kept insisting that I grab his hands, which I did not. Thankfully, the front door was open and my colleague returned. I introduced him and the man asked him as well, but he also didn't

---

[2] Recall the story of Fr. Verlinde, who got involved in a "Christian" esoteric group that used energy to perform healings. Fr. Verlinde never referred to this as Reiki. Hence, there are other very similar forms of this practice. See *The Rise of the Occult*, p. 285.

want to get energy passed to him. Then the man took off.

She said she works with a lot of different people from all different backgrounds and, up until that encounter, she had not felt uncomfortable around any of them. When she offered to pray with the man, telling him she is a Catholic and making the Sign of the Cross, he seemed very confused and became more insistent on touching her hands. When I mentioned this story to Barbara, who has an occultic background which included Reiki, she said this aggressiveness is actually not uncommon. She said, "Those involved even loosely in the movement are inclined to 'bless' and impart their healing touch on everyone and everything. Even when I was involved, I saw it as pretty arrogant and rude. People involved in Reiki have this tendency."

The woman in the above story added one thing that was very important. She said, "I am so glad I trusted my instincts and refused and had help from my colleague." "Going with your gut" and "trusting your instincts" is a repeated piece of advice from the people I interviewed. Our culture has been coaching us in the opposite in the process of breaking down all barriers and convincing the world to be accepting of everything, even the obviously weird, deranged, and evil.

Story: Family Division through a Reiki Spirit

A woman shared a mysterious run-in with her Reiki-practicing sister-in-law after having married into the family. This story highlights the diabolical quality to Reiki which sometimes comes to the surface.

I married into a family and the oldest girl (now in her 80's) learned Reiki at the Catholic college and became a Reiki Master. Before she even met me, she was telling her siblings/in-laws that I did not like her (I had not even met her!). I did not even know what Reiki was. She had used Reiki on my husband. Once, when I learned you could spray your home with holy water, I did that but not when my husband was home. The minute he walked in, the first words out of his mouth were, "It's those beads!" which I intuitively understood was a statement referring to my praying the Rosary, frequently, which had inspired me (I came to realize) to bless the house with holy water. My husband did not know I used the holy water, but it seemed that the Reiki spirit did.

Also, his Reiki Master sister point-blank, on the phone one day, and out of the blue, said to me, "Why don't you just go away!" I'm assuming it was the Reiki spirit that controlled her and it was not really her speaking. The Reiki spirit is, it seems, like most New Age religions, all about "self," not caring who you hurt on your way to improve yourself and glorify yourself. The control of the individual by the spirits is very subtle in these cases. It is difficult, though, because I don't know really how to handle the problem so I just pray for them. I guess it is as simple as this: Pray the Rosary and you are influenced by God; practice Reiki and New Age religions and you are influenced by the world and New Age spirits.

Chapter Seventeen

Yoga is a Dangerous Occult Practice

Occult practices today are diverse but are also quite united, ultimately containing the same message and overlapping in their purpose and essential techniques. Most people miss this and end up starting with one but drifting into many others in which they never intended to be involved. Yoga is one of these and this needs to be known: it is a technique quite compatible with all forms of occult practice.

Hatha Yoga, the predominant form of Yoga in the West today, was originally founded in the eleventh century by Matsyendra and Gorakshanath, two immoral individuals who used their yogic abilities to pursue their own disordered pleasures. Modern Hatha Yoga was crafted by a man named Krishnamacharya just over a hundred years ago. Based on Hatha Yoga, his form of Yoga spread throughout Europe, Asia and the Americas, and he was responsible for molding many of the most well-known and influential figures in modern Western Yoga.

Alex Frank, a former Yogi who is now a Catholic speaker against the dangers of the practice, bore witness to the occultic lure within Yoga. He began what would turn into a deep practice of Yoga simply from a desire to obtain relief from pain associated with back problems. He was already open to Eastern spiritualities at the time, but he said he could feel Yoga feeding an attraction to something deeper, something more, but he originally denied that in himself. "Yoga is clearly a gateway to a lot of New Age things," he said. Yoga is not only a gateway to New Age practices, he added, Yoga also generates "a magical attitude." It all begins with exercise but the real reason for doing this, Frank said, is "to start being able to manipulate energy and gain power over the movements in the body. When you add breathing to this, it gives you more power. Then, meditation gives you more control." Frank estimated that ninety-five percent of Yoga studios in the West are dedicated to what is known as the "left-hand path" style, a path that is less careful and without sufficient moral constraints, in which the practitioner will go into their "dark desires" to enhance them for the benefit of their own "consciousness." It is based on the attainment of power and is willing to transgress boundaries for the sake of attaining that power. The *right-hand* path, on the other hand, is the Yoga of a more structured traditional Brahminical Hinduism. It is like a monastic Hinduism, Frank said, "where scholars carefully write down what must be done and set up a correct ethical structure for the disciples to follow." This, he emphasized, is *not* the Yoga that is embraced in the West today.

Despite this predominantly left-hand path affiliation, most practitioners don't take it as far as they could but stay at the surface level. Frank added, "Though they stay on the surface, with the focus on the exercises, the effects of the Yoga on them are not good." Fr. Verlinde shared a story, from his time decades ago when he was a practicing Hindu, that demonstrates this reality. One day, he told his guru[1] that he had observed that Europeans practice Yoga purely for relaxation and not as part of a Hindu liturgy as it is intended. As Fr. Verlinde recalled, "He began laughing furiously, thought for a moment, and said, very significantly, 'But that does not prevent Yoga from having its effect'." The effect of Yoga is totally opposed to what a Christian should desire, which is to be focused on the other and on developing a personal relationship with the other. Within Yoga, Frank said, practitioners are learning to become subjectivist, self-indulgent, and focused on their own internal energies. Therese, who embraced Yoga throughout her decades of occult practice, said, "Yoga is selfish and gives the illusion of being *selfless* and open to love and compassion. The nature of it and its practice is selfish and inward. Yoga was the hardest thing to give up at my conversion." This aspect of Yoga gives even the surface-level practitioner the ability to manipulate those energies.

Part of the Yoga experience also involves mental coaching by an instructor. Yoga is not simply about how to do asanas (specific body postures) properly. "Generally," Frank said, "most are doing more than fitness." This "more" is understood by former occultists.

---

[1] Maharishi Mahesh Yogi, the Yogi of "The Beatles."

Yoga is a Dangerous Occult Practice

Andrew utilized Yoga in the beginning of his practice of Thelema, in addition to other breathing techniques. "You start small and get control over your body," he said. There are multiple degrees of involvement in Thelema, but practitioners start here. With the help of Yoga, they seek to prepare their mind and body for further and more demanding rituals. "Yoga breathing exercises and postures," he added, "were part of preparing for various magickal[2] practices in Thelema."

Frank also shared his insights about important figures in the Yoga movement. He pointed to Norman Sjoman, a Yoga scholar who practiced and studied under the 'father of modern yoga,' Krishnamacharya, who had stated, "What makes something Yoga is not *what* is done, but *how* it is done." This is particularly relevant given that most of the asanas of modern Yoga come from Western gymnastics and are not actually native to Hinduism. As this Yoga scholar indicated, it is not the asanas themselves that are the focus but the way the practitioners are using them. This breeds "a Yogic philosophy." The intent of Yoga is to participate in the spiritual process of Yoga, which is a yoking of the self to the Hindu spirits. Judith Lasater, who, Frank said, is probably the most prominent yoga teacher in the US, agrees with this understanding. According to Lasater, "Even if your concept is, 'I'm just teaching people how to stretch,' the intrinsic nature of yoga is that you cannot separate the asana from other aspects of practice. The well-being of the student-teacher relationship is dependent on the teacher's understanding that you're not the same as someone who simply teaches people to play the guitar."[3]

For Christians to consider embracing Yoga is for them to embrace a contradiction. Christian Yoga, Frank said, is an oxymoron. Literally, "Christian Yoga" would mean "Christian yoking to Hindu spirits," which is ridiculous. "Yoga," Camilla explained, "is antithetical to the Christian walk." The purpose of Yoga, "is to attain enlightenment through chakras,[4] through postures. These," she added, "have metaphysical or psychic

---

[2] Some occultists use this spelling to distinguish between occult ritual magic and a stage performance.

[3] *Yoga Journal*, August 28, 2007, "Gods and Monsters."

[4] A Hindu concept in which there are specific locations within the body where energy resides and can be trapped. Yoga attempts to release these energies.

ramifications that are not understood in the West." She stated that she has seen negative consequences in the practitioners' lives — emotional, spiritual, and physical. "The point," she said, "is to raise the kundalini energy from the base of the spine where the goddess Shakti the destroyer lives, which rises up to 'destroy ego,' but a lot of other things are destroyed in the process." "The real goal of Yoga,"[5] Adam Blai stated, "in its original context, is to awaken the kundalini spirit, which is a serpent[6] at the base of your spine that, over time, with enough yogic practice, will rise up your spine until it reaches your crown chakra [in your head], at which point…the evidence of this great spiritual awakening is called a *kriya*, which is what? Involuntary twitches and body motions with animal-like vocalizations that are out of your control. I'm not kidding," he said, "You can go *YouTube* this and see videos of it, both people [for whom] it's out of their control and people that think it's the greatest thing since sliced bread."[7]

The effort of "Christianizing" Yoga *normalizes* Yoga, which makes Christians think the Eastern spiritual elements are good. As a result, they are no longer on guard against these and the things with which these are associated. Former occultists and practitioners of Yoga experienced this themselves and warn about this danger. John said that Yoga is a practice that prompts you to unwind yourself and to see yourself not so much as an individual but as a part of the whole. "Everything is connected" is a basic perspective in Yoga, and this, he said, is important to take note of: it is echoed throughout the occult and pagan religions. "A danger of Yoga," Therese added, "is that the 'openness' it forms within you makes you primed to hear, and to listen to, this same message coming from occult groups who use the same language." Yoga weaves this language, these principles and perspectives, into the mind of the practitioner, even if the Yoga appears to be a non-religious type. At that point, the individual is more open and disposed to hearing these same things from other cultures that are not Christian, developing an attitude of acceptance

---

[5] *Yoga Journal* confirms this in their article on August 26, 2010, "Feel Your Full Bloom: Lotus Pose," where it states, "One aim of a hatha yoga practice is to awaken kundalini energy."

[6] *Yoga Journal* describes Kundalini as the "sleeping serpent goddess" in their article on August 28, 2007, "Yoga Poses for the Chakra System."

[7] Blai video.

toward foreign religious concepts. One consequence of this, she said, is to adopt the belief that "we are all connected, so there is only *different* but not *right and wrong,*" a common and pervasive form of religious indifference plaguing Christians today.

When these connections are understood, it becomes clear that today's Yoga is introducing people to things that the occult in general embraces in its various systems, such as energy centers (chakras) and key finger positions for meditation. Conditioned by this, if a practitioner of Yoga sees a New Age group pop up which presents the same external mannerisms, they will become very curious, especially if their form of Yoga has convinced them that they are on a spiritual journey for which Eastern meditation provides the best support. One of the problems is that some of the externals in Yoga, and those same externals in certain New Age groups, are not discussing the same spiritual realities. While both are oriented toward a spiritual framework incompatible with Christianity, the neo-pagans and the New-Agers who embrace Yoga for personal benefits will be led into the more dangerous practices of the occult by this overlap of language and external practices. Therese warned, "Neo-pagans [who simply dabble with Yoga] will go into Wicca and the occult; Yoga is a gateway drug."

Example: Yoga Leads to Occult Off the Mat

The best and most well-respected guide for modern Yoga is the group called *Yoga Journal,* according to Frank. As internet traffic statistics reveal, this is the most popular online guide to Yoga for Americans, even though most Americans are not Hindu. However, *Yoga Journal* serves as a reference point for lots of women and men who are now post-Christian spiritual seekers which, one could reason, is a very high number. The dangers are many, but one article makes several points very clear. This article also demonstrates the realities warned about above.

From *Yoga Journal,* the same group that published an article encouraging its followers to actually "call on Kali,"[8] comes this article from October of 2008, titled "How to be Fierce," in which the author told a story of when she advised another woman, whom she

---

[8] *Yoga Journal,* articles, October 9, 2015, and October 17, 2008, among others.

called "Annie," "to find your Kali side." The author stated that Annie, like many, often focused only on the stress-reducing aspects of Yoga and was unaware that "as you go deeper into your yoga practice, it will ask you at some point to confront those parts of yourself that may be suppressed." Enter Kali. Who is Kali, though? According to the author, in art she's "the one with wild hair, the bare breasts, and the severed heads around her neck...She's usually described as the goddess of destruction, and she looks scary, even though her face and body are beautiful." As if there were any doubt, the article clarified, "As an archetype of divine femininity, Kali is miles away from the image of Mary, the sweet intercessor."[9]

Revealingly, the author stated, "What Annie was about to discover is that Yoga can bestow gifts that are often obscured by our efforts to 'be good' – like bringing forth repressed passion and purifying it into *energy*, or *accessing* sublimated anger and wisdom that, when owned and *channeled*, can renew the body and lead to more-skillful actions."[10] Take note of the key occultic terms used in her description. After accepting the invitation to call on Kali, "[Annie] felt that Kali helped her hold strong" in resolving the difficult situations which prompted their initial conversation. The author of the article, when she was dealing with a health issue, said that she decided "to start a process of dialogue with what I...saw as my own suppressed Kali energy." To do so, she embraced a form of occult channeling known as automatic writing, though, of course, she did not give it that label. With her dominant right hand, she wrote, "I would like to speak to Kali," and then, with her left hand, she held the pen and began to write. It was no mere writing, for, she said, "I felt a leaping in my heart and saw these words flowing through my pen: 'I am angry, I am power'." She then asked, with the pen in her right hand, "What do you want?" to which she received the left-hand response, "I want out, to be free! To be wild! To be in control!" She described the process in these terms: "I could feel myself swinging from wild exhilaration to resentment and back again, but always with a feeling of mounting energy and excitement."[11]

---

[9] *Yoga Journal*, October 17, 2008. "How to Be Fierce."
[10] Ibid. Emphases mine.
[11] Ibid.

Yoga is a Dangerous Occult Practice

This article demonstrated many aspects of the danger of Yoga. Annie, who simply practiced Yoga for the reduction of stress, but was likely open to different religious ideas, was being instructed, likely unknown to her, by someone who summons the demon Kali as part of her spiritual walk. Further, this instructor believed that Yoga will eventually demand more from you than simply the external exercises. Once this instructor was able to offer direct advice to Annie, Annie summoned the demon as well and experienced tangible "assistance" from this spiritual and Yogic force.

Chapter Eighteen

Covid and Demons

"I could not dream up a scenario that would be this damaging."
Fr. Ambrose

There is no doubt that one of the most negative spiritual players to recently afflict the world is what has become known as, and has been associated with the term, *Covid.* The problem of Covid is not simply the virus that was unleashed on the world, and which has wrought havoc globally for almost four years; it was the response of the world and the Church to the virus which was the biggest evil. Churches were closed, schools were closed, businesses were closed, the internet became the "real world" for the majority of the population of the entire planet, the youth became isolated and depressed, people were left distrustful and confused regarding their sources for news and medical information, and a totalitarian mindset infected political leaders globally.[1] All of these are direct factors in the enduring state of depression and disillusionment afflicting not just the youth but many other age groups as well.

Exorcists are quick to call out the numerous evils that have emerged or have been strengthened during this reign of terror. Fr. Anselm said that he believes we will see a lot more of the occult emerge within society as a result of Covid.[2] "Covid was a big cause," he said, "because people were without the Sacraments since Churches were closed. The more distanced from God, the more people will turn to other things. The problems don't disappear, the issues don't disappear. If they are not turning to God then they are turning to something else, and the next closest thing, besides technology and sophisticated medical breakthroughs, is the occult. The occult also looks and sounds like the rituals of the Church. People are more

---

[1] See *The Rise of the Occult,* p. 115 for a related discussion.
[2] The reference to "Covid" here, and throughout the book, is inclusive of not just the virus but also the world's response to it.

susceptible as a result of Covid. The last few years[3] have been a wide-open door for this activity." Father added, making an important point, "They think they are turning to God by some other means; few are turning directly to the devil himself."

"Our best protection is our relationship with God, which has been crumbling for decades," Fr. Ambrose said. In discussing the impact that Covid has had on the faithful, he added, "Covid was one of the final nails in the coffin. The worst thing was for Churches to close; they are our greatest protection, and they take them away? That wreaks havoc." Felicity said that the combination of terrible catechesis and the reign of terror during Covid combined to drive lots of people away from the Faith. "People also left under Covid because they were not catechized well," she said. "They came just to feel good, have coffee after Mass, socialize, but we were not teaching people *why* they should be coming to Mass."

Fr. Ambrose pivoted to the imagery in the story of the Gerasene demoniac to make a strong point on the degree of the spiritual crises we are currently witnessing. Division, nudity, lying, and violence, as seen in the story of the Gerasene demoniac,[4] are calling cards of the devil, Fr. Ambrose advised. "When you see these together," he said, "there is a[n evil] power there." These were all on full display during the time of Covid: the lies spread through the media about the situation and the needed solutions, the division and isolation of individuals from families and society and the Church, the violence and riots rampant in the US culture and global oppressive government tactics, and the pornography distributed freely to the world by one of the leading distributors on the internet. In the midst of this evil chaos, all the Churches were shut down as well. "It was very much like a chastisement," he said, adding, "I could not dream up a scenario that would be this damaging."

It was not simply a situation of evil in the natural realm. Fr. Ambrose told his bishop about his observations as an exorcist, stating, "This is insane. Something is happening in the spiritual realm. Demons seem to have more power. But it makes sense: more sin *feeds* them. People are isolated and in a bad place as a result, and [are] doing bad things." It is important to note that *many* exorcists

---

[3] This interview was conducted in 2022.
[4] The possessed man in Mark 5 whom Our Lord delivered from a "Legion" of demons.

noticed this increase in evil. It was first publicly addressed by a group of four anonymous exorcists, who called on Catholics worldwide to pray and fast in order to mitigate the spiritual damage that resulted from the Pachamama idolatry in the Vatican in October of 2019.[5] This awareness continued deep into 2022, as my interviews revealed. "It seems that the demons are becoming much bolder," Fr. Alphonsus said. "There was a real clear discernment years ago, by exorcists, about something 'big' coming."

Fr. Alphonsus went on to explain that one of the "seers"[6] they use, who has a gift for spiritual discernment, can hear the diabolical "chatter" constantly. What she heard was bragging among the demons. When she said this, the deliverance team asked her, based on what she had been hearing, "Is Covid demonically influenced?" "Yes," she replied, explaining, "This is what they have been bragging about for over a year, that something big was going to happen, that would affect the whole world, and this was it." The seer said the demons, ever since Covid hit, seem to be more "off the leash" than she had ever seen. She sees them swarming around people, particularly the demons of obsession, anger, lust, and gluttony. The people the demons are "swarming around" usually have clearly opened a door to the diabolical.

It makes sense, given the above, that there may be a diabolical quality to the Covid virus itself, as many exorcists have speculated. I told Fr. Ambrose that it was reported to me that a hospital priest chaplain had great success using deliverance prayers to bring about remarkable recoveries in people suffering from Covid. He agreed it would be a good thing for a priest, especially one serving as a hospital chaplain, to pray deliverance prayers over someone with Covid. He does so anytime he is suspicious of someone having a diabolical influence and has never had a negative reaction. The only possible "harm" he said it could cause is if it frightens the person. So, prudently, he often does these silently since, as he said, "I am [already] in constant prayer when speaking to someone."

---

[5] *National Catholic Register*, November 12, 2019, "Four Exorcists Urge Day of Fasting, Prayer and Reparation Dec. 6."

[6] A seer, in this case, is a layman who has been recognized by the local Church to have a spiritual gift. These gifts vary. See Chapter Twenty-Two for more details.

Chapter Nineteen

Sage Smudging: A Widespread Occult Ritual

A very common occultic practice in the US culture, and throughout the world, is that of sage burning, also known as "sage smudging." It involves burning dried sage leaves and utilizing the smoke to "purify" the "energy" of a person, place, or item. Its occultic intent is to drive out the negative energy and bring in positive energy. It has no basis in reason and science and is, thus, superstitious. This practice has become so commonplace that people do not even realize it is superstitious or part of occult rituals. Christopher said that the burning of sage, the practice intended "to 'spiritually cleanse' a house, is absolutely ubiquitous." Most people are likely unaware of this practice before reading this book but, given how widespread it has become, his warning is important: "I don't think most people realize that burning sage is like putting a sign on your home that says, 'Demons Welcome'." In addition to being gravely sinful, it is a dangerous practice: exorcists have noted that diabolical attacks emerge as a result of the superstitious burning of sage.

What's Behind Sage Burning

People who burn sage in homes say it "purifies the atmosphere," spiritually speaking, but Fr. Cyprian said, it instead creates a portal to diabolical activity. He emphasized that, like the Ouija board, among other practices, it is the act itself which leads to these problems. In some stories of diabolical oppression, people have told him that they blessed their home with holy water and then burned sage in the house. When he expressed his shock and surprise, particularly if these were Catholics, their explanation, reflecting their deep ignorance on spiritual matters, was something as simple as, "Yeah, the neighbors said to do that."

The person that puts sage bundles together for smudging casts spells on it, Philomena emphasized, stating that she herself did this on many occasions. When this is done, she explained, there is some sort of intention placed on the sage bundles through the incantation. This is tied to the requested magical assistance by the person who paid for the sage bundle. Sometimes, a hair from the person is placed in the bundle and the spell is supposed to attach to that person. Helena said that, in her coven's rituals, after they would worship the goddess, "the area would be purified with sage and then each of us would purify each other with sage." This was due to the danger the goddess posed, and to reduce the threat of unwanted entities entering their "circle of protection." In one of the videos of the online witch Lola, in which she discussed a certain aspect of witchcraft, a viewer left the following comment about sage. It is very enlightening and troubling. Occultists see the effects of sage burning and, without discernment as to the diabolical agency at work, they celebrate the practice:

> I came into the office one weekend to do a little sage cleansing. I'd hoped to remove some of the negative energy that had been lingering and return a sense of joy to the office. Well, turns out that year we had our highest turnover ever because person after person quit. It wasn't my intention, but it did ultimately release the negative energy when they took it with them.[1]

Another comment said, "I've actually heard that burning sage is like spiritual 'bleach.' It removes all energies, good and bad." To that comment, a viewer responded, "Yep, that's why it's best to use sage alongside other things to help draw in positive energy after." Sage,

---

[1] This is one of the dangers of the occult. *By the agency of demons*, things do appear and occur. The agency of demons is the problem, for recourse to them is seriously sinful and they will eventually destroy, in one way or another, the person who called on them. The correlation here between the sage and the turnover, of course, cannot be proven to be caused by the diabolical, and we should hesitate to believe that to be the cause. Ultimately, all things that happen in our lives are within God's permissive will and under His governance and guidance.

as an irrational superstition, is often accompanied by other superstitious beliefs and practices, as seen here.

Sage Smudging in the Church

In 2022, *LifeSiteNews* reported on the increased exposure of children to sage smudging ceremonies in Catholic schools in Australia, as a result of what appears to be a global push to embrace indigenous religious rituals following the infamous Amazon Synod and the worship of the Pachamama idol in Rome. Australian exorcist Fr. John Rizzo said he had been contacted by three families in the course of two weeks whose children were suffering from the "unpleasant consequences" of attending these "smoking ceremonies." Symptoms have ranged from anxiety, irritability, and moodiness to "a type of fear that is hard to understand."[2] The mother of one of the children impacted by diabolical harassment after being forced to attend these rituals described her son's inexplicable inability to sleep in the following way:

> My son is naturally quiet, and he was at first unable to explain the reason for his inability to sleep. He eventually told us that about a week before, he had been visited in the night by a shadowy figure which screamed at him and pinned him down to the bed. When my son started to pray, the figure went away.[3]

In this case, and in other similar cases, Fr. Rizzo reported that a minor exorcism,[4] in addition to an increase in other standard Catholic devotions, was sufficient to bring an end to this diabolical attack. Exorcist Fr. Michael Shadbolt said that these smoking ceremonies are akin to tarot cards and casting spells and can cause the practitioner to be adversely affected in the same way. Fr. Rizzo and Fr. Shadbolt both said that these rituals are sins against the First Commandment and a form of idolatry.

---

[2] *LifeSiteNews*, September 1, 2022, "Exorcists warn of rise in demonic activity following Indigenous Pagan rituals."

[3] Ibid.

[4] Simpler prayers than the full Rite of Exorcism, which can be said by any priest, which ask Our Lord to drive out any activity of the Evil One from within a person or place.

This issue, of course, is not limited to Australia. *LifeSiteNews* also contacted Fr. Ripperger's Doloran Fathers, based in the US, on the issue. A representative said that "they have come across multiple instances of spiritual harm resulting from smoking ceremonies and other rituals used by the indigenous people of the United States as well as from those of other cultures."[5]

Story: Sage Smudging and a Diabolical Infestation

The following story was related to me by Cecilia, a devout Catholic wife and mother.

Cecilia went away with her family on a vacation and hired a pet sitter to watch their dogs and cats. The pet sitter was not Catholic but was great at the job. The family had lived in the house for several years and had already used this pet sitter on a few occasions. For whatever reason, this time a few strange things occurred while they were away. First, she received a phone call from the pet sitter stating that the house alarm was on. The odd thing with that statement is that the alarm system was not actually hooked up in the house but was simply still in the house from the previous owner. In order to get it to stop, they had to unscrew the panel and leave it hanging from the wall where it had been installed a long time ago. That report was just one isolated "odd" event at that point in this story.

In the first week after returning home, Cecilia was sitting at her desktop computer by the front door. The computer sat against a half wall between the desk and a hallway. While she was typing, she began to hear a strange and atypical rattling noise. She thought, "What is that and where is it coming from?" Not knowing what it was or what to do, she simply ignored it. The next day, she heard the same thing. This time, she attempted to locate the source. It appeared to be coming from *inside* the half wall itself. There was a picture on the wall that would rattle when the noise was present, so her husband went up into the attic above the wall to check and see if it might be the heating system and, hopefully, obtain a natural

---

[5] *LifeSiteNews*, September 1, 2022, "Exorcists warn of rise in demonic activity following Indigenous Pagan rituals."

explanation. Still not finding a cause, her husband checked the crawl space as well, to no avail. This sound kept occurring regularly, every day, for about three months. They could hear the sound but could not see where it was coming from.

One night, however, when they were sleeping in their bedroom down that same hallway, she did something that she came to believe caused an escalation of what appeared to be a diabolical presence: she decided to kick her husband out of the bed due to his excessive snoring. As she herself discerned and stated, "I was being a bad Christian wife." Looking back, she said she should have just gone somewhere else herself or used ear plugs.[6] Early that morning, she was lying on her left side and suddenly felt that she could not move. "It was terrifying," she said. She tried to push against the bed but could not move. The same presence that was preventing her from moving was also trying to suffocate her, she said. She struggled to say a *Hail Mary* and the *St. Michael* prayer and, once she did, she suddenly experienced a feeling of freedom. She was panicked and sweating and "completely freaked out." She prayed again (she could not recall which prayer) and then lay down again, not realizing exactly what the entity was. Then, she explained, "From under my pillow, I heard every curse word in the book screamed into my ear." She jumped out of bed, screamed, and ran. Immediately getting her husband, he returned with her with holy water and blessed salt and, along with a simple binding prayer, prayed for the evil thing to leave.[7] She eventually learned that demons, after having been granted permission to harass someone, sometimes manifest at night in a manner similar to this.[8] For her, the sensation it brought was

---

[6] This is an important moment. To *her*, this act was malicious and motivated by selfishness. It is not clear that this would have been a mortal sin, though she considered it to be a sin of some high degree. Thus, her action appears to be connected to the demon's ability to harass her further. Permission to harass a person is not granted to demons in a strict "cause and effect" manner, since God blocks most of what demons want to do to us. Two people may commit the same serious sin but God may only permit one to be afflicted in some way by a demon while the other remains unaffected.

[7] A binding prayer such as: "In the Name of Jesus, I bind you, spirit of evil, and cast you to the foot of the Cross to receive your sentence," or, simply, "Jesus, I ask You to bind any evil spirits who are present within my home," etc.

[8] This permission, as presented in *Slaying Dragons*, is connected to a mortal sin or occult activity of some sort, and must also be permitted by God, since demons do not have the right to harass us whenever they want. God, by His own power, and by the activity of His angels and His saints, blocks them the majority of the time.

that of a pillow being pressed over her head, followed by the slew of vile words. It took a few days for her to put it all together and understand what was happening. She also noticed pretty quickly after this event that the wall was no longer vibrating. A few more details then emerged that would shed a more complete light on the matter.

In a conversation with the house cleaner, who was a friend of theirs, she found out that the house cleaner was in the home on one occasion when the pet sitter was also there. The house cleaner told her that she had seen the pet sitter bring in a sage smudge stick to "clear the air in the house." The pet sitter was going throughout the whole house with it. The house cleaner thought that this was odd but did not know what, if anything, needed to be done about it. Cecilia began to understand the situation in the following way: once the demon was brought into the home by the pet sitter, it hung out in the wall (a typical infestation) until she acted in the manner that she described as "being a bad Christian wife," at which point the demon received permission to attack her. The demon was then angered after being thwarted by her initial prayers and attacked her again with the cursing. After she and her husband entrusted themselves to Our Lord, sprinkling holy water and blessed salt and saying binding prayers together as a couple, the demon departed, and no other issues arose. Having lived through this experience, and after putting the pieces of this puzzle together, she was left with absolutely no doubts about the diabolical nature of the event.

When she finished the story, she added that she thinks the pet sitter was well-intentioned and did not expect any trouble to be caused by the smudge stick. This is highly likely the case since, as has been presented in this book and *The Rise of the Occult*, most people are completely clueless about the evil and danger of the superstitious practice known as sage smudging. That being said, the danger and damage remain. To this day, Cecilia said she still has trouble even uttering the words "smudge stick" when telling this story.

Chapter Twenty

The Occult in the Marketplace – A Tale of Etsy

Etsy, the "global online marketplace, where people come together to make, sell, buy, and collect unique items," is also a marketplace for occultism. It once fought against the occult's presence in its marketplace. Now, however, Etsy appears to have caved to the prevailing culture. Etsy is a good case study for the current state of our culture.

In 2012, eBay (not Etsy) changed its rules and banned the sale of spells, hexes, healings, potions, and the like from its platform. As a result, witches flocked to Etsy, which became one of the most popular places for these "metaphysical services," which were allowed so long as the "services" were accompanied by a tangible item. In 2015, though, Etsy also changed its rules, prohibiting the sales altogether, even if the seller still provided something tangible. Apparently, Etsy had moved quickly and began shutting down shops that did not comply with the new guidelines. This caused a great uproar and made the news on all the major networks. Witches were annoyed and perplexed by the change, especially since Etsy had been very welcoming to the witch community up until that point. Many witches began to believe that they were being targeted as a result of a religious bias against occultic activity. Many Christian religious items were still permitted, which the witches said was proof that Etsy was guilty of religious discrimination. When the news of the change and the complaints became public, Amazon reached out to the witchcraft shops and invited them to set up their shops on their new *Handmade* platform. Though it still exists, Amazon Handmaid does not appear to have been a great success. Still, there are now over nine thousand options under "spell supplies" on Amazon.

Six years later, Etsy, despite its rule change, was still allowing witchcraft shops. A Reddit thread from 2021 discussed the fact that, despite the ban on such things, there were spells everywhere, and official categories were also provided for them on the Etsy platform. "Metaphysical services may not be sold in our marketplace," Etsy currently states on its website.[1] You can sell a tarot reading so long as it comes with a tangible item, but you can't cast spells or do rituals for someone which promise a specific metaphysical outcome. At least, this is what they *say* is the rule.

Early in 2022, another online discussion about the presence of spells on Etsy, despite the ban, theorized that Etsy had simply made a truce with the witches. Etsy is so overwhelmed by the number of shops that are open and operating against the rules, that they simply cannot police them all. It reminded me of Neo from *The Matrix*, who, in the third movie, made a truce with the machines, but did not liberate humanity from them. Neo and humanity entered into a "coexistence" with the evil machines *for the time being*. But good cannot *tolerate* evil; the evil will corrupt the good and take over. Etsy tried to cancel the sale of spells seven years ago in order to preserve some sort of integrity. It makes one wonder: have they read the "signs of the times" and are now convinced that the occult is mainstreamed and unstoppable?

Currently, in 2022, spells are aplenty on the Etsy platform. Putting "spell" into the Etsy search bar today will bring up a huge inventory of spells that are all one click away. The visitor to this search result will be greeted by numerous disturbing images and even offers of "death spells." There are over two hundred thousand different services offered under the search word "spell." There are likely even more out there that come up under different key search words. Further, in the category "Witchcraft Shops," there are just under six thousand different shops.

What Kind of Spells?

Searching for "death spell" (yes, that's correct) will bring up close to three thousand different options.

When the visitor looks at a "star seller" of "death spells," it is bewildering, to say the least. The comments are filled with accolades like "[the seller] is so nice...goes above and beyond...a nice

---

[1] As of 2022.

person...so willing to help...very patient," to which the seller responded in equally kind and gracious words. All the while, he is casting spells for them that seek to cause "death," achieve "revenge," cause "annihilation," and manifest "hate." The seller is clear in his description that he uses black magic "and demons" to cast his spells.

Looking at the comments for an "obsession spell," the witch in question is clearly effective in her spell work. She received high praise for her helpfulness and accuracy. Her spells apparently work, or at least every appearance is there that they work.[2] Looking at the description of the shop, she is clearly doing "spellcasting," in violation of the literal Etsy rules, but she stated at the bottom of her page, in order to skirt any violation, "Due to the terms and policy, I am stating that [sic] is for entertainment purposes only." Clearly, everything else in her description proves the contrary.

So, what are we to make of this? Witchcraft has its foothold in the culture. There is now clearly a market (literally) for it – an audience and a revenue stream. Stores that once desired to resist it can do so no longer. And what does that lead to? The young generations are growing up in an ever-increasingly "witchy" world.

This reminds me of a question I once posed to an exorcist:

Do you think it's possible that the religion of the Antichrist could be witchcraft and the occult? And that we could eventually see pentagrams and other occult symbols everywhere, like Christian symbols used to be?

Answer: *Definitely.*

---

[2] One technique of the diabolical is to give the *appearance* that spells work in order to convince the witch, and the one consulting the witch, to continue the practice.

Chapter Twenty-One

Horror Movies? It Depends: A *Case-by-Case* Analysis

In my interviews with former occultists, one of the items we discussed was horror movies and films loosely within that category. Could any good be drawn from them or are they, as a whole, harmful? Christopher provided a comprehensive list of concerns: the lack of theological accuracy which these films contain, how they are easily confusing to uncatechized viewers, their inclusion of immorality and blasphemy, their presentation of gore which can truly scar the mind, as well as the fact that they create an adrenaline rush which, in the context of a presentation of the diabolical, "can breed sympathy for the devil." While everyone I interviewed sided with issuing a caution against watching horror movies, this came, at times, with a disclaimer. John, for example, said that, if an occultist stumbled across the rare horror movie, like those of the *Conjuring* series, which portrays these things more accurately, it could be an occasion for a spiritual awakening. These positive potentials, however, were deemed to be only narrowly possible.

The presentation of evil and the diabolical in a show or movie will vary, affecting the morality and danger of watching it. Helena said that it really depends on the show. "Some will scare you into staying far away [from the occult] and others will glamorize it," she said. Andrew agreed that it is a mixed bag. The presentation of the diabolical in horror films can have positive and negative aspects, he said. He noted that one movie, *Hereditary*, used the name of a real demon as the central antagonist in the film. He said it also used real occult symbols from the same grimoires and books he was using in the occult. As a result, Andrew declared, "I will never watch that movie." Certain shows, like *Sabrina*, mock and twist the Catholic Faith and present Satan as a substitute for Our Lord in the process. It also downplays the evil of fraternizing with the devil. All of these can subtly undermine the Christian intellectual framework in a mind that is neither well-catechized nor spiritually formed to detect the devil's deceptions.[1]

Benefits of Horror?

Conversely, some films, while still potentially disturbing, could have a positive impact on the viewer, all things considered. John pointed to the movie, *The Shining*, as an example, stating it does not glorify the diabolical but makes it clear that the spirits in the hotel were evil. This clarity, John said, is important. Andrew spoke similarly, "The portrayal [in horror movies] of demons and the occult as objects of malice and evil, and of priests and the Church as good, is probably okay." The issues of catechesis and a well-formed conscience remain a concern, though. He added to that, saying, "Though, again, someone with a malformed conscience and lack of proper catechesis should likely avoid any exposure whatsoever."

Andrew argued that there is a place for horror in films today given a certain aspect of our culture that he has observed. He said, "We are disconnected from death today, unlike centuries ago. There is a place for horror in film, so long as it is not the blasphemous sort. It makes people fear death, which people avoid even discussing today. We need death *in our face* more. Priests could easily do that in homilies but they don't. However," he added, "the people in charge of these symbols in movies are not on the side of Truth and the Church." As a result, an important opportunity to educate properly on death is not only missed but inverted, causing harm instead of sounding a salvific alarm.

There are some films, though, that are still keeping the traditional truth about good and evil. John again drew attention to *The Conjuring* films, based on the true story of the Warrens, a Catholic couple permitted by the Church to work in deliverance ministry and who did so for decades. "These films present a very Catholic universe to the viewer," he said. While some people – including this author – will still not want to watch these films because the mere presentation of the diabolical can be disturbing, John pointed out that this kind of "horror movie" would be good for

---

[1] For one commentary on *Sabrina*, see ChurchPop.com, November 10, 2018, "Netflix's 'Sabrina' Mocks Christianity, Glorifies Witchcraft & The Demonic."

people in the occult to see. "It fills a void and a need for real good and real evil," he said, adding, "It would provide for God to work in a place you would not expect."

Abiding Danger

Though there can be some good things that come as a result, there is still a danger in watching these presentations of evil. According to Philomena, "The more you see them, the more they desensitize you to the occult." One show, for example, *Supernatural*, is about two brothers who hunt demons. They use symbols throughout the show. As a "fandom" grew, she said society began to see these symbols everywhere, including fans getting them tattooed on their own bodies. In the show, they speak in Latin as they perform "exorcisms," and fans use these Latin expressions as ringtones on their phones. "However," she pondered, "do we even know what is being said in Latin in these ringtones?" The show *Sabrina*, which, she says, is "blatantly Satanic," and *Lucifer*, which depicts Satan helping solve murders, are both examples of shows which, if viewed regularly, can desensitize the viewer to the reality of evil. As she put it, "Once you become numb and don't feel the evil of it, the damage is done."

When someone is so interested in a movie portrayal of evil, Christopher advised they should reflect on *why* they are so interested in watching those movies and *why* they find the occult, wizards, sorcery, and demons so interesting. If it is not "for the greater glory of God," which it likely is not, then it is for morbid curiosity; and therein lies the danger. Fr. Amorth voiced his concerns about horror movies, saying, "[These films] tend to normalize brutal situations, particularly, where the demon is the protagonist" and "can seriously upset fragile minds and stir others to sadistic emulation." He added that, though viewing these films does not directly cause spiritual ills, they can indirectly do so by enticing the person who watches them toward the occult.[2]

The presentation of evil in stories such as in fairy tales, John pointed out, used to provide lessons about the reality of good and evil in the world. "There are monsters in this world and you will

---

[2] Fraune, *Slaying Dragons*, 159.

need to fight them," fairy tales proclaim. Early horror films used to keep this dimension in the story, even depicting the good people as the ones who survive and the bad people as the ones who fall victim to the evil. Catholic priests would regularly appear as part of the solution. "Now," John said, "it is like 'horror porn,' evil triumphing over good and leaving the characters in a state of despair." Good is losing and the characters have no recourse to truly protect themselves. They either try to fight off the evil on their own or turn to a pagan culture for the solution; but they're always losing, and evil is always winning. As John said, "It is starting to become a trend in film."

One of the deceptive illusions is that demons are good and that vampires, who used to be viewed as monsters, such as in *Dracula*, are today depicted as glamorous and glittery, ready to be your friend or even your romantic interest. Fr. Thomas saw this same danger in the show *Lucifer*. One of his concerns is that shows like *Lucifer*, which present the devil as a likeable individual, are encountered by the youth in an age of hyper-gullibility. Kids look things up online and often believe something to be true *simply* because someone wrote it, with no further discernment. The absence of rational thought and critical thinking is mind-boggling in this age, he said. Further, the religious void in which the youth are growing up has robbed them of a proper sense of religious authority. So, this sort of show is being accepted by the youth in such a way that it prompts them to ask openly and honestly, "What if Lucifer is not that bad?" The danger of such ignorance is really unimaginable.

Chapter Twenty-Two

Spiritual Gifts and the Occult

Within today's religious seeking, people today, inside and outside of the occult, talk about *gifts* and *giftedness*. In Catholicism, this typically reflects a good and wholesome desire to do good to others. We know that Our Lord bestows supernatural gifts that are then to be used in the service of the Church. These gifts are quite various and, while many are listed in Sacred Scripture, that list is not exhaustive. In the occult, there is also talk about gifts. These occultic gifts are not always intended to be used in the service of others. Often, these are special *abilities*, such as astral projection, seeing the future, reading hearts, seeing auras, directing good energy to someone, directing negative energy toward or away from someone, healing an illness, performing a sign or wonder, and having control over spirits.

In this list, there are *some* gifts that have a resemblance to those bestowed by the Holy Spirit, as the Church has seen and approved. With the rise of occult practice and diabolical activity, in an age of godlessness and a spiritual void from the dying of Christendom, individuals today are seeking and celebrating *gifts* in ways that do not always receive the discernment they demand. As a result, individuals take hold of these supposed gifts and make themselves into a sort of *magisterium*, a self-originating religious authority, one which has no anchor in God or in truth and is, thus, primed for deception.

An American exorcist highlighted that extraordinary gifts of the Holy Spirit are not necessary for salvation and, as a result, we should not seek them nor even desire them. They are a *gift* and cannot be merited or attained through any method. One of the dangers today is that, in the occult, people are seeking to *attain* spiritual gifts through various methods. These gifts are not such as would come from the

Holy Spirit and this should be clear to them; they are sought through diabolical agency or through communication with the amorphous and unnamed realm of spirits and energy.

Some of the gifts that are reported by occultists, as mentioned above, have a parallel in those given by the Holy Spirit. Saints have been reported to have the ability to read hearts or read souls, to foretell the future, to levitate, and to perform various sorts of miracles, including healings. Exorcists have worked with mystics who can see demons, detect which kind of demon is present, see how many demons are present, see where the demon is present, understand how the demon got into the person's life, perceive the wound by which the person became open to the demon, "bear the burden" of another's spiritual suffering and detect what that suffering truly is,[1] see demons that are attached to pictures, see angels, and recognize a true relic over a fake one, among many others. Devout and sound-minded faithful have reported similar abilities as well as the ability to "read" people and become aware of what they can only think to call "auras."

As we know, the devil mocks all that is holy and seeks to create a counterfeit version of the True Faith. The devil, possessing an angelic nature, also has the ability to perform certain signs and wonders, to do amazing things in this world and in a person's body and mind, all of which, while appearing to be miraculous, are simply a power intrinsic to his angelic nature. This deceptive power of the devil is not to be underestimated. He is capable of deceiving even would-be Saints; he is surely capable of deceiving anyone who does not stay anchored in the Church and in the virtue of humility.

What Exorcists See

Some exorcists will bring gifted individuals onto their exorcism teams. These individuals are sometimes referred to as seers, sensitives, or simply *gifted*. From the experiences of exorcists, the gifts that these individuals have received from God are typically related to the activity of the diabolical. There are a great many more gifts that exist in the life of the Church, but those gifts did not come

---

[1] Msgr. Rossetti blog, April 3, 2022.

into focus in my conversations with exorcists and my present focus on the rise of the occult.

One exorcist, Msgr. Rossetti, has spoken a lot about his work with gifted individuals. He has stated that there are many kinds of gifts and that exorcists particularly appreciate those who can sense the presence of demons and even the kinds of demons present.[2] He emphasized that, yes, while most gifted people sense the presence of demons, there are a few rare individuals with the ability to actually see them.[3] In one exorcism session, Father was attacked by the demons and was made to feel nauseated. The gifted person in the room was able to tell him, before he shared the nature of the attack, that she had seen the demons attacking him, and described exactly what Father was experiencing. "Gifted people, or spiritual sensitives, have a God-given charism that helps them to discern spiritual realities, often including the presence of demons."[4] "Some mystics," he said, "have had visions of Hell and noted that demons beat up the humans in Hell. It's massively ugly. But demons beat each other up too."[5]

Msgr. Rossetti explained what often happens to a gifted individual in a situation like the above. He said, "One of the ways our gifted team members know that demons are present is that they themselves quickly get a headache and a feeling of nausea when the affected person enters the room; the stronger the demonic presence, the stronger the symptoms. In really bad cases, the gifted person can hardly stand being in the same room."[6] Father added that these individuals often experience the same level of exhaustion that the exorcist experiences after a difficult exorcism session, which can sometimes last several days.[7]

Fr. Bartholomew observed that the people he has encountered who possess gifts of discernment have experienced significant suffering in their lives. He understands that these gifts are present as a "gift" as a result of their patient endurance of trials. Those gifts have included the ability to read a room, see the state of souls, and

---

[2] Rossetti, *Diary*, 53.
[3] Ibid 48.
[4] Ibid 29.
[5] Ibid 41.
[6] Ibid 213.
[7] Ibid 48.

even a supernatural sense of smell. Fr. Sebastian said that some of the gifts he has observed included a greater sensitivity to seeing and hearing things on the spiritual level.

Fr. Alphonsus said that one woman who was once liberated from the diabolical now works with exorcists. She has the ability to see demons on pictures and on screens, which, as he said, is something that is happening these days. She can tell what kind of demon is present,[8] and what level in the demonic hierarchy it occupies. "A seer like that is very helpful in ministry," he added. She can tell the exorcist the exact location of the demon in the room or in the person's body.[9] The exorcist can then pray directly over that spot and will notice a huge change in the demon's behavior, indicating she was correct.

Fr. Alphonsus also told a story of a Catholic husband and father, with young children at home, who works on a deliverance ministry team. Because of his work, he has had to endure demons in his home on a regular basis. His children have had the ability to see the demons and to show the exorcist exactly where the demons are located. Children like this usually lose the ability by the age of four or five and forget all about it. "Thank goodness," Father quipped. Sometimes, though, a child will retain the gift, indicating that it might be permanent. Msgr. Rossetti agreed that children can often see angels and demons more easily than adults. He said that, when they lose childhood simplicity, this ability often leaves as well.[10]

Fr. Alphonsus added an interesting detail about these gifts. He said that some people with gifts have a difficult time controlling them. One seer, who could read people's hearts,[11] would walk into a room and immediately have knowledge of the people present. She eventually learned how to turn off this gift. An interesting detail here is that witches discuss a gift that sounds very similar to this. They refer to this as being an *empath*. The witch Lola defined an empath as "someone who can feel another's emotions as if they are your own." This is very similar to Fr. Alphonsus' description, who said an *empath* can "feel the emotions of everyone in the room as if

---

[8] "Kind" here refers to what type of sin it primarily instigates.

[9] Since they do not have physical bodies, demons are present in a place by their activity there.

[10] Rossetti, *Diary*, 57.

[11] Not minds but hearts – an important distinction.

they are their own." This includes "the anger of some, the stress of others, the sadness of others." Lola said that it is often an overwhelming experience and not everyone thinks it is a positive thing.

The seer who could read people's hearts once told Father exactly what his homily was about at a specific weekday Mass despite the fact that she was not present at the Mass nor had any knowledge of what he preached in his homily. She said she had been able to see it on his heart at the prior Sunday Mass. "To her," he said, "our hearts scream out. If there is something someone is really concerned or excited about, it screams out to her."

Fr. Alphonsus knew of another person whose inability to turn off her capacity to see demons created problems for her. She told him, "The more the demons know that you know that they're there, the more they act up and intimidate and cause problems." She eventually developed the ability to turn it off and, in consultation with her spiritual director, decided that using this gift was too much for her and she stopped it altogether. The more she had allowed the gift to operate, the more she suffered.

Fr. Alphonsus shared that there was one time that he asked one of the gifted individuals, a seer, to hold different relics in her hand to see if she could tell if they were authentic. This was not done out of curiosity but because of some confusion about the authenticity of the relics. One was a relic of Padre Pio which Father was hoping was authentic. When the seer held the relics, some did not give her any special sense, but when she held the Padre Pio relic, she said a warmth was emanating from it. This kind of manifestation was confirmed for him when speaking with Fr. Carlos Martins, an exorcist who leads the group *Treasures of the Church*, which travels the world with over one hundred and fifty relics, giving schools and parishes a chance to learn about and venerate them. He told Fr. Alphonsus that people attending the display of relics have had a similar experience of sensing heat coming off of the relics when they venerated them.

One seer, named Felicity, told me she has had spiritual gifts since she was little. From a young age, she could see things on a spiritual level that no one else could see, but it was so frequent that she thought everyone saw them as well. It was only after attending a retreat sponsored by Charismatics that she came to understand just how God wanted her to use that gift. Now, she works with exorcists and deliverance ministry teams to help identify what, in the life of a troubled individual who has sought their help, is at the root of the individual's spiritual suffering. This enables the priest to more quickly address the problem and bring about a liberation from whatever form of diabolical harassment the individual is undergoing.

Spiritual Gifts in a Family

Ava's mother informed me that she herself has a certain spiritual gift which it seems highly likely that Ava, currently trapped in the occult, also possesses and uses. She can look at a picture of someone, or look at someone in person, and can tell certain things about them. They will have an "air" about them, something about them that is difficult to explain but is not based on outward appearances. She will, for example, have a horrible feeling about someone, like a sixth sense, or a sense that they are a very holy person. She is not really sure what the gift is or what to call it, but it is a real thing.[12] She spoke to Ava about this and found out that Ava has the same ability and can do the same thing. As a result, it seems that Ava is using the gift in combination with being a life coach. The mother counseled her that she can use this gift to lead people to Our Lord. Ava said that her ability to read people is uncanny and people find it astonishing. Ava also said she is unsure about this gift and her ability to read people often scares her.

Gifts Perverted by Demons

Fr. Alphonsus commented that these gifts can be given by God or by the devil. One man who was possessed had also had an uncanny gift of occult knowledge but, when he was liberated from the demon, he lost it completely. That is a clear indicator that it was from the devil. Others, however, will retain the gift even after being liberated. If that is the case, it is meant to be used to help souls, possibly in service to the Church in association with the exorcists and deliverance ministry team in the Diocese. There is one theory about these gifts which states that some *gifts* are natural gifts,

---

[12] This individual is a prudent and holy woman.

residual gifts from before the Fall of Adam and Eve, and are thus best referred to as *preternatural* gifts, rather than *supernatural.* This is written about in the book *Occult Phenomena: In the Light of Theology* by Abbot Alois Wiesinger. The latter is referenced by Msgr. Rossetti in his own book, as well as by other exorcists. Fr. Thomas provided the following example in support of this concept: "The psychics who assist law enforcement are not *necessarily* involved in occultic practices or using diabolical sources for their information. They might be using preternatural gifts in the sense of 'pre-lapsarian' gifts that survived the Fall or are supplied as a gift by God." The Church has no teaching on this matter but recourse to prudent and educated priests is recommended for anyone who thinks they may have such a gift.

It is also possible, he said, that the devil can seek to take one of these natural gifts and pervert it to a selfish or occultic end. Fr. Anselm said that the devil could try to destroy or manipulate these gifts in people who are outside of the Church or dabbling in the occult. These gifts, he said, must always be at the service of the Church and connected to the Church. Fr. Sebastian agreed and pointed out that these abilities are attractive to demons, who seek to pervert these gifts or cause the person to use them for their own personal benefit, whether financial or to increase pride. These gifts must always be seen as a gift which God desires to be used to help others, useful to the Church as a ministry through which God can help people in special situations. "It is not a career," he added, "nor about getting paid for these services. Charging a price or a fee – that crosses a line."

A Danger: Occult Use of Gifts

In my conversation with Fr. Thomas about the issue of gifts, he shared some interesting insights. In his ministry he has observed the reality of gifted individuals who can, for example, see deceased souls.[13] From his pastoral experience, he said, "It happens; it's real. It can happen through dreams or while awake, but the evidence for its

---

[13] The issue of "seeing dead people" is debated among exorcists. Human discernment of such an apparition must be done very cautiously due to the potential for demonic deceptions. While an apparition may appear as, and truly be, a "soul from purgatory," it could also be a demon seeking to deceive the person.

authenticity is convincing." When people engage with these gifts or sensitivities, they are engaging with something they do not totally understand, something which they cannot always tell is being honest with them. Once people perceive that they have such a gift, they often naturally try to develop a system for understanding it. Whether the gift is natural or by the working of the devil, it can nevertheless easily be *mis*understood and can turn the person toward the creation of a false religious worldview.[14] Father said people begin to develop a religious worldview around these sensitivities because their search for understanding deals with things that reside beyond the material world. "This is where it gets very dangerous," he said. "The authority we need in order to assemble the proper image of the eternal is rooted in Christ and His Church. This has to guide these people as well. If someone is having a genuine experience with a natural gift, the danger emerges when they begin to ascribe more knowledge and insight and religious authority to these things than they deserve."[15]

Getting to the most dangerous aspect, he said, "This is where it can lead people into the occult.[16] They begin to piece together a worldview with religious assumptions that go unquestioned. They believe that everything they experience is an honest experience, that they have the ability to discern what it means, and that anything that happens in these experiences is honest and good. The biggest danger is [presuming to understand what] you cannot know and understand in this realm without religious authority. In the natural order, reason is sufficient, and no revelation is needed. In matters that go beyond the natural order,[17] revelation and authority is required. These people are giving the same authority [to their gifts and experiences] that we give to natural things backed up by reason. In the end, [they] make the experiences, or themselves, into the

---

[14] Here, he is not referring to special gifts, or charisms, from the Holy Spirit, which accompany a life of holiness and are more intelligible, though always mysterious, to the individual Christian who receives them.

[15] For example, cases where religious sisters get into Reiki and then "progress" beyond Christ.

[16] The Monroe's daughter, Ava, as mentioned earlier in the chapter, believes, in one part of her occult practice, that she is using natural gifts she possesses, rather than occult powers.

[17] Witches believe magic is part of this world and thus natural. This can blind many occultists and lead them to think that the powers they are dealing with, and desiring, are not subject to a religious authority outside of themselves.

religious authority, and they build a religious landscape that is false. We do the same thing when we reject certain doctrines simply because we don't like them. However, we, like they, are not fonts of revelation and we don't have the authority to decide whether something is eternally true or not."

Chapter Twenty-Three

The Power of Sacramentals to Block Occult Activity

The sacramentals of the Catholic Church are known to have, as one of their chief effects, the ability to block the activity of the devil. Holy water, famous for this grace, is not the only sacramental with this gift from God infused into it by the blessing of the priest. Blessed salt, blessed candles, the St. Benedict Medal, and the Miraculous Medal, among many others, are also known for this effect. These sacramentals are utilized by exorcists within the Rite of Exorcism and when assisting the faithful who are dealing with other forms of extraordinary diabolical activity. Further, repeating the admonitions of the Church, these sacramentals are recommended by exorcists for the faithful to make use of in various ways as they make their way to Heaven.

The application of sacramentals, such as holy water, blessed salt, and the medal of St. Benedict, in the lives of the faithful has many forms.[1] In addition to the common practice of sprinkling holy water and blessed salt throughout a home, and of placing medals within the home and on the land, one exorcist has recommended that parishes, when dealing with a strong intrusion of the occult, can bury blocks of blessed salt in the four corners of the property. This, as a practical measure, ensures the prolonged presence of the sacramental along the edges of the parish property. As a result, it would act as a further deterrent to the diabolical who may seek to stir occultists toward that parish with intentions to desecrate it in some manner.

With this understanding of the power of sacramentals to block the activity of the diabolical, many have wondered, in an age where the occult is on the rise, how else the faithful may employ these

---

[1] See chapter ten of *Slaying Dragons* for more on sacramentals and their use by the faithful, including a wonderful story (p. 136) of St. Teresa of Avila's experiences with holy water.

blessed items to block the activity of the occult within the culture itself. As answers to this question emerge, we must always keep in mind that the power of these sacramentals flows both from the Church's blessing as well as from our devout use of them. Faith, as seen in Our Lord's earthly ministry, unlocks the power of His grace and allows it to flow into our lives in real and tangible ways. As a result, many wonder if it is proper for Catholics to place sacramentals in areas where occultists may gather, such as was done a few years ago at a location to be used by Satanists the following day.[2] There is also the question of whether placing sacramentals in the homes, or beneath the beds, of wayward children may also prove to be efficacious. A priest's prudent answer to this question was that, if these sacramentals are used *with devotion* by the one who places them in that location, then it would not be superstitious. Other priests hesitate and regard this as potentially superstitious. In the end, sacramentals are gifts for the faithful to increase the presence of God's activity in their lives. With this in mind, Catholics, as members of the Mystical Body of Christ and, in that sense, extensions of Christ into the world, do bring the action of the Holy Spirit into the world by this divine union, producing miracles and healings and the conversion of pagans. The use of sacramentals would, as a consequence, naturally assist in this work.

There are many examples in the history of the Church of the use of sacramentals to block the activity of the occult. As mentioned in *The Rise of the Occult*, around 1871, Bl. Bartolo Longo, who was once a Satanist, returned to his old group of occult friends one last time after his conversion:

> A bold approach to reaching out to occultists was taken by Bl. Bartolo Longo. After the restoration of his soul, he was filled with such gratitude and he decided that he must seek to save the souls of his friends who were still lost in the occult. Bravely, he attended one more séance in order to renounce the occult in the presence of his old friends. He stood up in the middle of the ritual, renounced those occult practices as a

---

[2] TFP Student Action. "Satanic Temple Event Hits Big Wall of Prayer." *YouTube*, 20 February 2022, youtube.com/watch?v=9R1vg5y4HDg.

"maze of error and falsehood," and held up a medal of Our Lady for all to behold. From that point forward, he dedicated himself to prayer, in particular to a devotion to the Rosary and Our Lady.[3]

While there is no report as to whether or not the presentation of this sacred medal by a man of great faith had any impact on his old friends, the use of the medal in this way is indicative of the belief that such an influence was possible. The Miraculous Medal, just a few decades before this moment in the life of Bl. Bartolo Longo, had been demonstrated to have the power to convert occultists. The name itself, "Miraculous," was given to the medal as a result of the wonders the Church beheld upon its integration into the lives of the faithful. The famous case of Alphonse Ratisbonne, ca. 1841, who was both a Freemason and an atheist, gave much credibility and fame to the new sacramental. After accepting the medal from his friend and having just a slight bit of openness to the power of Our Lady to work through the use of the medal, Ratisbonne was blessed with an immediate and powerful conversion to the Catholic Faith which led to his eventual ordination to the priesthood.

As also mentioned in *The Rise of the Occult*, a famous Eastern monk, known as Elder Paisios,[4] demonstrated the power of the sacramental of the Cross to break the hold which the diabolical had on a powerful occultist:

As Alex recounted, Elder Paisios witnessed the boy's occult powers, including his ability to walk through walls. The boy then exclaimed, taunting him, "Can *Christ* make you do these things?" "No," Elder Paisios said, repeating, "but Christ can make you *not* do these things." At that point, Elder Paisios was permitted to put a wooden cross over the boy's neck and the boy immediately lost all his occult powers and abilities. Apparently, the boy also had a personal demon and, after he started praying with Elder Paisios, and staying at the monastery, the demons would beat him

[3] See *The Rise of the Occult*, 325. Mary's Dowry, Bl. Bartolo Longo documentary, YouTube.
[4] Paisios was canonized by the Synod of the Ecumenical Patriarch in 2015, so he's now St. Paisios the Athonite.

up to prevent him from progressing spiritually with the monks. In the end, the boy stayed and became a monk himself.[5]

In an old book on the various uses of holy water by Rev. P. Canon McKenna, an important story is related about the power of holy water to block the activity of the occult. From the lives of the Saints, we know that holy water has the power to drive away manifestations of the devil and block his ability to harass the faithful. This story shows the further power of holy water to interrupt the operations of the diabolical within the world.

As Fr. McKenna related, a priest from the Order of the Redemptorists was giving a mission in a certain city where it was known that a meeting of spiritualists was being held. When the bishop heard of it, he sent one of the Fathers to prevent the evil spirits from exercising their influence over their mediums. The Father went in disguise to the house where the meeting was to take place. He took with him a bottle of Holy Water. Before the performance began the Father sprinkled the whole floor with the Holy Water. The medium, a young woman, soon came upon the stage to get into a trance but could not succeed. They tried for about an hour but got no answer. At last, the performer – the medium – said: "Ladies and gentlemen, we have to give up tonight. There must be present some opposing power, as the spirits do not appear nor speak."[6]

An almost identical story was told by Fr. Dom Prosper Guéranger in his book, *The Medal of St. Benedict*:

> In 1839, a celebrated magnetizer, who had performed several wonderful things in different towns in France stopped at [a town], where he advertised that he was going to give public performances. He took about with him to all these different places a young girl on whom he exercised his mesmerism, and he drew crowded audiences by the extraordinary effects he produced on

---

5 Fraune, *The Rise of the Occult*, 261.
6 Very Rev. P. Canon McKenna, P.P., V.F. *Holy Water: Its Origin, Symbolism, and Use* (Sensus Traditionis Press, Casper, WY, 2022), 26.

this poor victim. In the town of which we are now speaking he attracted an immense crowd by his advertisement. The lecture was to be given in a very large room, which anciently had been a church, but had been turned to profane uses long before this. The hour came; but nothing that the magnetizer did, had the slightest effect, and the girl remained unmoved by all his passes. The audience was dismissed, and the money returned to those who grumbled at being disappointed. A few hours after, placards were plastered up all over the town, announcing a second meeting, at such an hour, in the Town Hall. This time also, the lecturer could do nothing, and after all his trouble and expense, he stole away from the town. Next day came the papers with their scientific explanations of the failure. One would have it that the room had been too hot, another that the gas was too much turned on, and the rest. Of course, none of them assigned the true cause. A nun who had happened to hear of the proposed lecture, knowing that the Church is opposed to the practice of mesmerism, resolved on thwarting the operations of the lecturer, so far as they had any connection with the devil. All she did was to hang out of her cell window a Medal of St. Benedict and beg the intervention of the holy Patriarch. Thus, the result was what we have related and the prince of the power of this air, as the apostle called Satan, was vanquished.[7]

Sacred Scripture provides insights into the power of grace, flowing through sacramentals, to interfere with the working of the occult. In addition to seeing Our Lord's power, which He bestowed on His Apostles, working against the devil in cases of possession, we have the account of St. Paul destroying the occult power of a slave girl who was used by her owners as a means of income. When a priest drives out demons by the power of Christ, he is performing what the Church calls a sacramental. Sacramentals also include the

---

[7] Edward Van Speybrouck, *Miracles of Father Paul of Moll* (Caritas Publishing, 2017), 248-249.

blessing of a priest. In this account, St. Paul wields his apostolic authority and, in the Name of Jesus, simply commands the demon to leave. This account is very similar to the above story, in which an occultist was utilizing a young woman in order to demonstrate his occultic powers and make money in the process.

> As we were going to the place of prayer, we were met by a slave girl who had a spirit of divination and brought her owners much gain by soothsaying. She followed Paul and us, crying, "These men are servants of the Most High God, who proclaim to you the way of salvation." And this she did for many days. But Paul was annoyed, and turned and said to the spirit, "I charge you in the name of Jesus Christ to come out of her." And it came out that very hour.[8]

The Church, whose authority is from the same Lord as that which St. Paul received, commands demons in a manner similar to St. Paul in this account. In the blessing of the medal of St. Benedict, for example, the priest states, "May [those who wear the medal] escape by Thy merciful help every onslaught and fraud of the devil," and, as the priest continues, "I humbly appeal to Thee to drive afar all snares and deceits of the devil from him who [uses this medal]." Thus, the one who devoutly uses this medal, such as the nun mentioned above, is essentially proclaiming to the local area these same commands, by the voice of the Church: "Begone, Satan, with every onslaught, snare, deceit, and fraud that you bring."

Witches Note the Mysterious Impact of Grace

Quite fascinatingly, online witch-YouTubers, in particular Lola, speak about their own experiences of spells appearing to be blocked or "bouncing back" due to the presence of various sorts of "protections" which exist on people, places, or things which are the target of a spell or curse. Listening to the wording, it immediately calls to mind sacramentals and their power, endowed by God working through His Church, to protect from diabolical activity the

---

[8] Acts 16:16-18.

one who devoutly uses the blessed item. "Devout use" is key because the sacred power of sacramentals is the love and mercy of God who freely distributes this grace to those who use these items out of love for Him. This point is critical to understand and incorporate into our religious practice since it both protects us from superstition, to which man is inclined by the Fall, and it *unlocks* the Heart of Jesus, so to speak, for we then love Him and receive His love, and love becomes an exchange of gifts.

From Lola's experiences, it is clear that the spells that witches send can often bounce back to the witch that sent them. There are many reasons for this, according to Lola. "It doesn't just have to be ancestors [who are protecting the person targeted in the spell]," she said, "It can be spirits in the area, it can be energy, spirit guides, it can be familial spirits, it can be demons and angels, and anything that's protecting them and shielding them." This list, from wherever she devised it, includes angels and "anything that's protecting them and shielding them." Perhaps that mysterious "anything" refers to the sacramentals and the power of grace, to which the occultist is blind as a result of her spiritual distance and disordered perspective. Lola perceived and acknowledged an opposing power in this "anything," in a way not unlike the Athenians of St. Paul's day who perceived and worshiped at the altar of "an unknown God."

Some of the more specific things Lola listed are "magical wards, protections, charms, talismans that are protecting them." She uses the terminology of witchcraft because, from her perspective, a sacramental would be similar to a charm or a talisman, though in reality fundamentally different. She also spoke about these same protections on people's businesses, property, homes, vehicles, etc., which block the spells, or "workings," and send them back to the witch. This is another reason to have all of these things blessed.[9] In case the reader is unaware, the Church supplies, and encourages us to receive, blessings on all of these things. The Church, animated by the Holy Spirit, desires to bless everything that we have and use.

One technique Lola suggested to other witches, in order to get around these protections, is instead to aim the spell at an *object* the

---

[9] The blessings the Church places on specific items imparts God's protection to the person who uses them devoutly. This protection can take many forms, such as the restoration of physical health, deepening contrition for sins, aiding prayer, and removing both the object and the one who devoutly uses it from the devil's reach.

person owns. This is important for us to know – this is how witches think and this is yet another reason to bless everything that enters your house and all food and drink you consume. Since the number of practicing witches is on the rise worldwide, this is prudent and is the course that more and more priests, and exorcists especially, are taking and encouraging: bless everything. Given the fact that the Church encourages us to bless our food before we consume it, both to give thanks to God and to ask Him to fill it with His goodness, it makes sense to ask God to bless all of our possessions. Consecrated to Him, they leave the domain of evil and are outside of the devil's reach.[10]

In discussing witches' ability to be protected from spells backfiring, Lola (erroneously) claimed, "Fellow witches and magical practitioners will have much stronger shields, protections, wards, ancestors, angels, spirits, whatever it might be that is protecting them." However, she went on to note that she has observed that it is "not just witches" who are protected.[11] Sometimes, she reported, "Just normal people, who maybe don't know anything about the magical and spiritual planes," are also protected. This, we can suppose, is the result of veiled interactions she has had with the operations of the Kingdom of God in the lives of Christians, and the protective mercy of God that operates in the lives of all men and women, since demons have no power unless God allows them to have it.

---

[10] One means of blessing everything we own is to consecrate our possessions to the Most Blessed Virgin Mary. This is an approach encouraged by Fr. Ripperger, as presented in *Slaying Dragons* (p. 65), as well as by Msgr. Rossetti. See the appendix in *Slaying Dragons* for a prayer which Fr. Ripperger encourages the faithful to use. A similar prayer can be found at the St. Michael Center for Spiritual Renewal > Prayers for the Laity > "A Prayer Against Financial Curses."

[11] As a clarification, as *The Rise of the Occult* and this present work have shown, witches are not in the least bit protected from the dangers of the spiritual world, except by the general mercy of God which blocks most of what the demons seek to do to all mankind.

Chapter Twenty-Four

Advice for Priests on Various Topics

The life of a priest today is becoming more complex as a result of the number of grave evils to which modern man is falling victim. This includes a great number of pathways into the occult or into a realm where the devil is very active and aggressive. This chapter is a collection of advice for parish priests that can help them navigate some of the varied situations which are impacting the souls who seek their assistance.

The Power of a Priest's Counsel

The priest who generously ministered to Bl. Bartolo Longo was the instrument through which this Satanist would be converted into a Blessed and become a great instrument of Divine Providence. Longo was introduced to the Dominican priest early on in his conversion process. This priest met with Bartolo every day for a month. On the Feast of the Most Sacred Heart of Jesus, the priest gave Bartolo, a former anti-Catholic Satanist, absolution and Holy Communion. Lucy also benefitted from a generous pastor. As a result, she was able to enter the Church by joining the RCIA with only a few weeks remaining before Easter. Priests have a greater power than they realize for counseling people away from the occult. Fr. Ambrose pointed out that every priest is already engaged in this sort of spiritual warfare, so it is easy and natural to expand what they are doing as the need arises. Highlighting that Our Lord's exorcisms are on par with His healings, Fr. Ambrose said, "In the confessional, the priest is already in spiritual warfare. So, he might as well be in it completely!"

Power of Prayer and Fasting

Many priests, following the lead of the modern Church, also do not understand the power of prayer and fasting. Fr. Ambrose addressed this issue passionately. "One thing that is important to take note of," he said, "is that the entire Church used to fast from midnight before going to Mass. During those times, we had a Church that was fasting on a regular basis." This fulfilled, as a Mystical Body, Our Lord's admonition that "prayer and fasting" was required in order to cast out some demons. "We don't have the 'prayer and fasting' that Jesus said is required to cast out some demons," he continued. "The hour-long fast is essentially nothing. Imagine," he continued, "all of that fasting, if the whole Church went back to that. Imagine the power!"

As was presented in *The Rise of the Occult*, Pope Ven. Pius XII taught at length the profound mystery of the nature of our union with Christ in the work of salvation. By this union, our prayers, good works, and sufferings truly matter and are a means of calling down many graces from Heaven. Among the many things he said on this was the following: "The salvation of many depends on the prayers and voluntary penances which the members of the Mystical Body of Jesus Christ offer for this intention and on the cooperation of pastors of souls and of the faithful, especially of fathers and mothers of families, a cooperation which they must offer to our Divine Savior as though they were His associates."[1]

Danger of Just a Little Dabbling

Fr. Cyprian told me the story of a woman, unprotected by sanctifying grace, with whom he worked who had only dabbled a little bit in Buddhism, beginning with an attachment to 'innocent' Buddhist memorabilia. However, this little dabbling that she did quickly introduced her to diabolical activity and brought serious spiritual problems. The lady he helped first began to have issues after returning from the Far East and with some Buddhist

---

[1] *Mystici Corporis Christi*, #44. See chapter Nineteen in *The Rise of the Occult* for more on this topic.

memorabilia.[2] When she got home, she began to hear voices. At the time, there were other disordered elements in her life, which opened doors for these spirits to attack. She also began to engage in conversations with these spirits, which was a dangerous decision that gave a strong sign of her consent to their presence. She was then taught by these spirits how to read the stars and open astral portals so she could see into the past and the future. She could read the star alignments and give messages to people, even randomly as she walked past them. "It was really creepy," Fr. Cyprian added.

During the deliverance sessions, Father said the lady's face would morph[3] and her head would turn in ways that were not normal. They also heard the names of the demons that were afflicting her and were able to trace those names through a network of exorcism and deliverance work to see what those demons were all about. There was one demon that was attached to her intending to destroy her marriage with her husband. In the process of working with Fr. Cyprian, she did a thirty-day prayer routine from the *Liber Christo* program, during which time the priests looked for any specific reaction to the prayers being said. This helped strengthen her and enabled her to battle against the attacks herself.

Buying Antiques

Based on warnings Philomena had once mentioned, I asked Fr. Alphonsus whether people should be careful about what they buy, with the idea that some items, especially antiques, might be cursed. Father replied, "I have had a number of people who have bought demonically possessed objects, particularly from antique shops and brought things into their homes. That's another whole area to warn people – if you buy something from an antique shop, have it blessed, have deliverance prayers prayed over it, because, depending on who it belonged to, it could be an object that could bring the demons into your home. I have had a number of people with problems like that."

Exorcists vary in their opinions about how worried faithful Catholics should be about items, such as antiques, that they

---

[2] As this account describes, the spiritual affliction cannot be tied with certainty to these pagan items. The woman's moral and spiritual life were already disordered and providing opportunities for diabolical harassment.
[3] See Fraune, *Slaying Dragons*, 81.

purchase. However, as Fr. Alphonsus said, he has had a number of people come to him with problems that appear to have originated from just such a thing. Similarly, Fr. Cyprian, as noted above, has also had to help people whose spiritual problems were potentially tied to an item which had diabolical attachments related to occult practice. The following account, from Christine, provides a further example of demons appearing to attach to items as a result of occult practice. In the following story, however, the reader should take note of several issues, as presented in *The Rise of the Occult*, which could have created other open doors to diabolical influence in her life. If these open doors and wounds are healed, and the life of grace and prayer and good works is established, a Catholic should then have little fear of the devil's extraordinary activity.

Christine and her sister Edith were raised in a broken home by a mother who was deep into the New Age. The mother permitted the two girls to play with Ouija boards and even sent them to psychics as if it were a gift. Before they were teenagers, they had both become victims of abuse. When they were young adults, they tended toward bad relationships and sought out the New Age themselves as a way to deal with the pain they had accumulated from such a life. Edith had gotten deep into Yoga and astrology and had committed two abortions before her conversion to Protestantism. Before this conversion, she had also begun to experience diabolical manifestations, experiencing diabolical attacks in her dreams and sometimes during the day as well. At one point after her conversion, Edith was giving away a lot of stuff from her apartment and Christine went over to visit. Christine saw a large mirror and decided to take it home, thinking it would look nice in her daughter's room.

A few months after taking it home, the daughter, around eleven years old, began to complain about not being able to sleep and of a "monster in the mirror." The girl had suffered from sleep issues, including childhood night terrors, for a very long time, so they did not take this complaint too seriously. However, this new complaint did not resolve and eventually the daughter began sleeping in the living room. Shortly before they had gotten the mirror, Christine had listened to a talk by a former Satanic priest, who had told the story of how he began his Satanism as a youth utilizing a mirror to conjure a demon. This former Satanist had also said that mirrors were often used in the occult as portals.[4] When Christine was walking by the mirror one day, in the midst of the daughter's struggles, "It just hit me!" she said. She took the mirror out of the room and tossed it in the dumpster. From that point forward, the daughter was fine and she no longer suffered from these new disturbances.

Cursed Images

Based on Fr. Alphonsus' report that a seer he works with was able to discern the presence of demons attached to digital pictures of individuals, I asked him if images could be another portal that people are blind to today. "Definitely," he responded, "especially with pornography." Pornography has been proven to be a pathway into the occult. Pornography, as one man told me, was also the doorway to a powerful same-sex attraction, just on a natural level, which burdened him for many decades before he found liberation through prayer and assistance from a psychologist. As Fr. Ripperger has reported, exorcists have been told that pornographers employ Satanists to curse the videos they produce, which Satanists have stated will travel with all copies of the film, even digitally.

Tattoos and Piercings

According to Fr. Alphonsus, a growing number of tattoo artists are now involved in the occult and have put cursed tattoos on people. Fr. Cyprian said that, when people come to see him for help, he always asks them about tattoos. He does this because he has learned that Satanic tattoo artists will curse the needles they use when they give people tattoos. One exorcist also stated that the ink used in some tattoos is known to have been cursed as well. In addition to these concerns, the tattooed image itself has to be evaluated for occultic connections.

To undo a cursed tattoo, there is a prayer for what is called "decommissioning tattoos" that exorcists, or any priest, can use to remove any curse or diabolical intent behind a tattoo, whether from the tattoo artist or from the person who requested the tattoo. It is a

---

[4] See *The Rise of the Occult*, 213 for a related story.

deliverance prayer which breaks any occultic connections, curses, or diabolical attachments that may be present on or in a tattoo. This is yet another way to redeem these occultists and give them hope that, despite the mutilation of their bodies by the tattoos, they can at least be spiritually restored to the dignity of a son of God. For tattoos that are clearly demonic, Fr. Athanasius recommends the use of the Rite of Reconciliation of a Profaned Temple (or cemetery), with the wording adjusted to fit the circumstances of the tattoo and the person's body as the object involved. In the process, the priest should use a Q-tip to paint over the tattoo with blessed oil.[5]

I asked Fr. Cyprian, "Would you recommend that anyone who has a tattoo, and is trying to live a holy life, and cannot remember anything about the tattoo artist, should go ahead and get the tattoo decommissioned?" He replied, "It wouldn't hurt! We sometimes use diagnostic tools to see if something works, in addition to the standard plan." Fr. Blaise said he once had to decommission a tattoo due to the demonic imagery it involved. "One man that I worked with," he said, "had a tattoo of a demon crawling out of his chest – that was a problem."

Similar to tattooing, multi-piercing is also a concern. "People with many piercings are people who often have psychological problems, and this is one of their ways of expressing it," Fr. Cyprian explained. "I would not be surprised if the demons used it to their advantage to get involved in the person's life because these are usually troubled people." People who get lots of tattoos or are multi-pierced are wounded, he explained, adding, "Wounded people are like catnip to demons – demons are drawn to them because they can just suck the life out of them, and attach to them very easily."

When I asked him about the practice of cutting, Fr. Cyprian said, "It is not only common but it's growing, particularly because, with Covid, so many kids are still psychologically so damaged and have so many problems. So, cutting among girls and even guys is growing from everything I can tell from working in a number of schools; it's becoming even worse." He said he has not observed cutting to be a doorway for the diabolical, but it could definitely be used in that way.

---

[5] Blessed oil from the traditional Roman Ritual, not that which is blessed during the Chrism Mass.

Demons Messing with Phones

In one case, as Father was making progress helping a man to relocate in order to get the help he needed, the demons began texting Father and also taking over his phone. The same thing had happened with someone to whom he was giving spiritual direction. Another exorcist advised him to type back prayers to the number texting him. "Apparently," he said, "the demons are very exposed when they text, so if you type back 'Our Father' or 'Hail Mary,' they stop." In this case, that is what happened. Demons will also call him or have possessed people call him. Msgr. Rossetti has also reported instances of demons messing with phones. Not only are they able to send texts, but they also block the technology from working. "It is not unusual," he said, "for possessed people to find it difficult to speak to their exorcist on their cell phones because of demonic interference."[6] Former occultists have also reported this same phenomenon.

---

[6] Rossetti, *Diary*, 102.

Conclusion

While the occult is clearly spreading and establishing deeper roots in the culture with each passing year, it must be remembered that the Church was established precisely for the purpose of destroying the works of the devil, of which the occult is a principal manifestation. In this troubled age, we must remember that God will never allow His Church to be removed from the earth or to be destroyed by her enemies. She, as the Mystical Body of Christ, has for her soul the Holy Spirit Himself. God is ever with His Church and is ever sustaining her and her faithful members.

As a result, the principal work of Christians today must be to fortify their union with Christ and His Church that they may bear fruit and so prove to be His disciples. It is through the pursuit of individual holiness, by which the divine life of grace will flow through us and into the world, that we will effectively work against the presence of the occult. Were the divine life to be inhibited from flowing freely in our souls, instead of bearing supernatural fruit we would be tending toward spiritual death. Should the divine life cease to flow as a result of unrepented mortal sin, we would be dead branches on the Vine. Dead branches, as Our Lord solemnly warns, cannot bear fruit.

Evil only wields a conquering power against those who do not love God and serve Him in this life. When Christians fail to preach the Gospel, pagans will remain firm in their disobedience and their attachment to sin. Conversely, when the Gospel is faithfully proclaimed and heroically embraced by those who bear the name of "Christian," the world will be drawn to the fount of salvation by the alluring aroma of the Truth.

This book has presented the stark reality concerning the lure and deception and spread of the occult in our world today. It is now up to those who profess to love God and, consequently, to love their neighbor, to find the ways in which they can shine the Light of Christ into the growing darkness of this fallen world. With Christ, we are victorious. Let us endeavor to recruit all whom God places in our paths into this eternal victory.

References

Blai, Adam. *Hauntings, Possessions, and Exorcisms.* Emmaus Road Publishing, Steubenville, 2017.

Ermatinger, Fr. Cliff. *The Trouble with Magic.* Padre Pio Press, 2021.

Fortea, Fr. Jose Antonio. *Interview with an Exorcist.* Ascension Press, West Chester, 2006.

Gallagher, Dr. Richard. *Demonic Foes.* New York: Harper One, 2020.

McKenna, P.P., V.F., Very Rev. P. Canon, *Holy Water: Its Origin, Symbolism, and Use.* Sensus Traditionis Press, Casper, WY, 2022.

Pratt, Sr. Antoinette Marie, A.M. *The Attitude of the Catholic Church Towards Witchcraft and the Allied Practices of Sorcery and Magic.* Washington: National Capital Press, 1915.

Rossetti, Fr. Stephen. *Diary of an American Exorcist,* Manchester: Sophia Institute Press, 2021.

Speybrouck, Edward Van. *Miracles of Father Paul of Moll.* Caritas Publishing, 2017.

Documentaries and Features

CheminNeuf NetforGod. "A Guru or Jesus Father Joseph-Marie Verlinde." *YouTube,* 20 June 2017, youtube.com/watch?v=kHoKWxp8Imo

EWTN. "EWTN on Location - 2019-10-26 - Allure and Truth About Wicca and Witchcraft (The)." *YouTube*, 26 October 2019, youtube.com/watch?v=FCf7JJ4w0dc; ["Blai video" in footnotes]

EWTN. "Scripture and Tradition with Fr. Mitch Pacwa - 2019-11-05 - 11/05/2019," *YouTube*, 5 November 2019, youtube.com/watch?v=Pea6aaSS8sw&t=2048s

Francisco Huanaco. "Is Wicca and Pagan the Same? Differences Between Wiccan and Neopagan." *YouTube*, May 25, 2020, youtube.com/watch?v=Vtln5rX2WMA

Jesus 911. "06 May 2020 The Most Evil Woman in the World." *YouTube*, 7 May 2020, youtube.com/watch?v=krLGDzFdbR4

Larson video #1 – Occult Demon Cassette. "The First Family of Satanism [VHS]." *YouTube*, 24 June 2014. youtube.com/watch?v=uRf-FyDfRY0

Larson video #2 – Satania. "Showdown with Satanism - Bob Larson Interviews Zeena Lavey and Nikolas Schreck." *YouTube*, 14 March 2020. youtube.com/watch?v=jfk9NZ5pgRw

Marysdowry. "Bartolo Longo, NEW FULL FILM, biography, power of the Rosary, Mary's Dowry Productions." *YouTube*, 30 May 2018, youtube.com/watch?v=3OQLRndbHIM (see also youtube.com/watch?v=NdR4bn2Bl-E)

The Nikolas Schreck Channel. "Nikolas Schreck Interviewed by Legs McNeil THE DARK SIDE OF THE SIXTIES PT 2 HOLLYWOOD SATANISTS," *YouTube*, April 17, 2022. youtube.com/watch?v=aIAqa-I0HjQ

Riaan Swiegelaar video #1, Facebook, July 4th, 2022. Accessed July 20, 2021. Video was taken down in the months following this research. Similar video here: youtube.com/watch?v=3g81MbTEw_Q&t=1630s

7NEWS Spotlight. "'SATANISTS NEXT DOOR' | Our cameras capture a secret ritual as a 'curse' is cast | 7NEWS Documentary." *YouTube*, 27 February 2021. youtube.com/watch?v=Wqa5F6vWWXM [Ciaran Lyons video]

Additional Resources

Summa Theologiae of St. Thomas
> http://www.newadvent.org/summa/index.html

Catena Aurea and Gospel Commentaries of St. Thomas
> https://aquinas.cc

About the Author

Charles D. Fraune is the founding Theology teacher of Christ the King Catholic High School in Huntersville, NC and was a Theology teacher there for ten years. He left teaching on the high school level to found the *Slaying Dragons Apostolate* as a result of the response to his best-selling spiritual warfare book, *Slaying Dragons: What Exorcists See & What We Should Know*. This Apostolate is dedicated to sharing the wisdom of spiritual warfare from the counsel of modern public exorcists in the context of the Church's two-thousand-year history of authoritative teaching on the subject.

In addition to the above, he has taught nearly every grade level, from second grade to adult, including on the college and diocesan level. He spent three semesters in seminary with the Diocese of Raleigh at St. Charles Borromeo Seminary in Pennsylvania. This completed a nine-year discernment of the priesthood and religious life after which he discerned that Our Lord was not calling him to the priesthood. He has a Master of Arts in Theology from the Christendom College Graduate School, as well as an Advanced Apostolic Catechetical Diploma. His enjoyment of writing began over twenty years ago and culminated in his first completed book, *Come Away By Yourselves*, a guide to prayer for busy Catholics. He has also written a spiritual warfare manual for youth and their parents, called *Swords and Shadows: Navigating Youth Amidst the Wiles of Satan*, and a companion book to *Slaying Dragons*, which serves as a workbook, study guide, and spiritual warfare manual, called *Slaying Dragons – Prepare for Battle: Applying the Wisdom of Exorcists to Your Spiritual Warfare*.

Find him at SlayingDragonsPress.com.

Slaying Dragons Press

Slaying Dragons Press, founded in 2021, is the fruit of a spiritual work begun in 2016 which sought to find new ways to bring people the joy and beauty of the Catholic Faith. By God's Providence, what began under the name *The Retreat Box* has grown into *The Slaying Dragons Apostolate* and *Slaying Dragons Press*.

This work is a grassroots apostolate which thrives on support and endorsements from those who enjoy these books. As a result, fans of the books and supporters of the mission help increase the reach of *Slaying Dragons Press* by telling friends, family, priests, religious, and Bishops about these books.

Please consider supporting this work in any way that you can. While *Slaying Dragons Press* is *not* a non-profit, financial support is always welcome. Please visit SlayingDragonsPress.com for ways to support this apostolate. If you do not have a copy of the other celebrated books we have published, get one today!

*Support this work on **Patreon!**
~patreon.com/**theslayingdragonsapostolate**

*Subscribe to the author's website for discounts and news!
~SlayingDragonsPress.com/pages/**Subscribe**

Popular *Slaying Dragons Press* Titles

The Rise of the Occult: What Exorcists & Former Occultists Want You to Know

Slaying Dragons: What Exorcists See & What We Should Know
(also in Spanish – *Matando Dragones*)

Slaying Dragons - Prepare for Battle: Applying the Wisdom of Exorcists to Your Spiritual Warfare

Swords and Shadows: Navigating Youth Amidst the Wiles of Satan

Come Away By Yourselves: A Guide to Prayer for Busy Catholics

Slaying Dragons Press

Made in the USA
Middletown, DE
02 March 2024

50681271R00123